The Renaissance House

By Robert W. Burns

Copyright 2012, Robert W. Burns

FOREWORD BY STEVE STONE

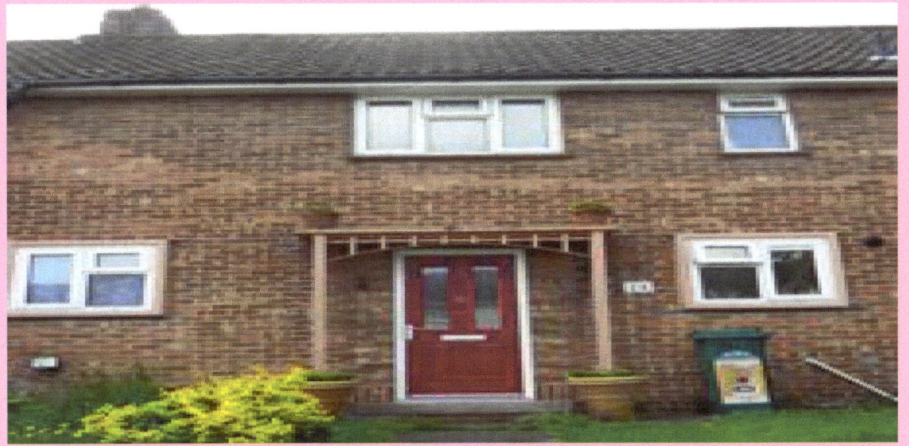

This looks just like any ordinary house, doesn't it?

But it's not an ordinary house. Not at all. This is the Brighton house of painter and decorator Robert W. Burns. On the outside, it seems like any other dwelling, but on the inside, it's been transformed into an incredible art gallery, a shrine to and celebration of Renaissance art, containing wonderful reproductions of classic works from centuries gone by; portraits, wall frescos, lunettes and friezes alike.

Just turn the pages - you won't believe your eyes. The house also contains original Renaissance-style portraits of Russell Brand and Wayne Rooney. Throughout the book, magenta text on pastel pink background pays homage to the most cherished colours of the Renaissance period.

As featured by BBC's 'The One Show', ABC, Channel 9 Australia and AFP. Certain images are from Robert W. Burns, others included by kind permission of legendary international photographer Facundo Arrizabalaga.

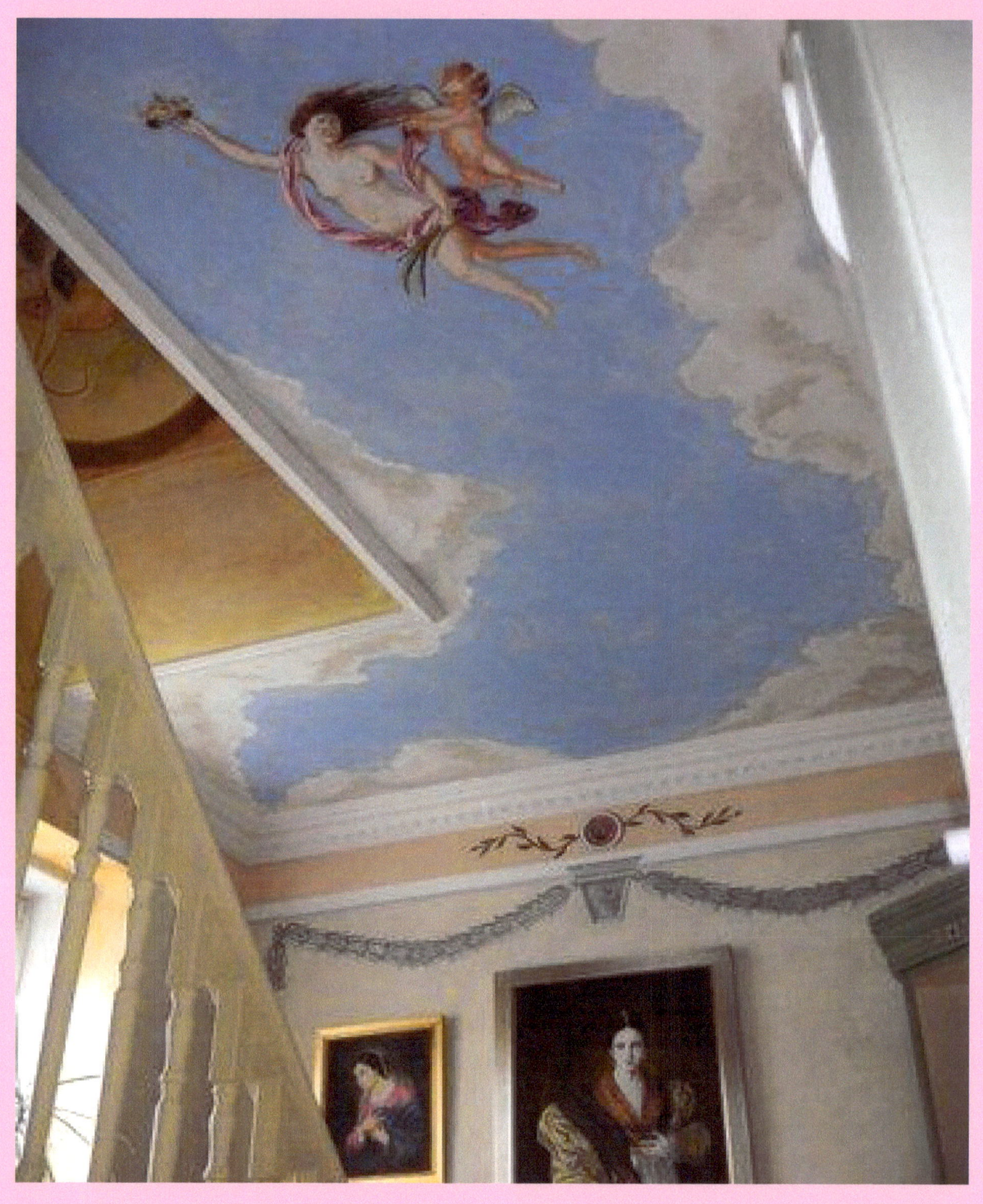

Hallway. The ceiling detail is taken from Guido Reni's 'Fortune Held Back by Love'. Reni (1575 - 1642) was an Italian painter and engraver, particularly renowned for his 1613 'Aurora' fresco at the Rispigliosi Palace, Rome.

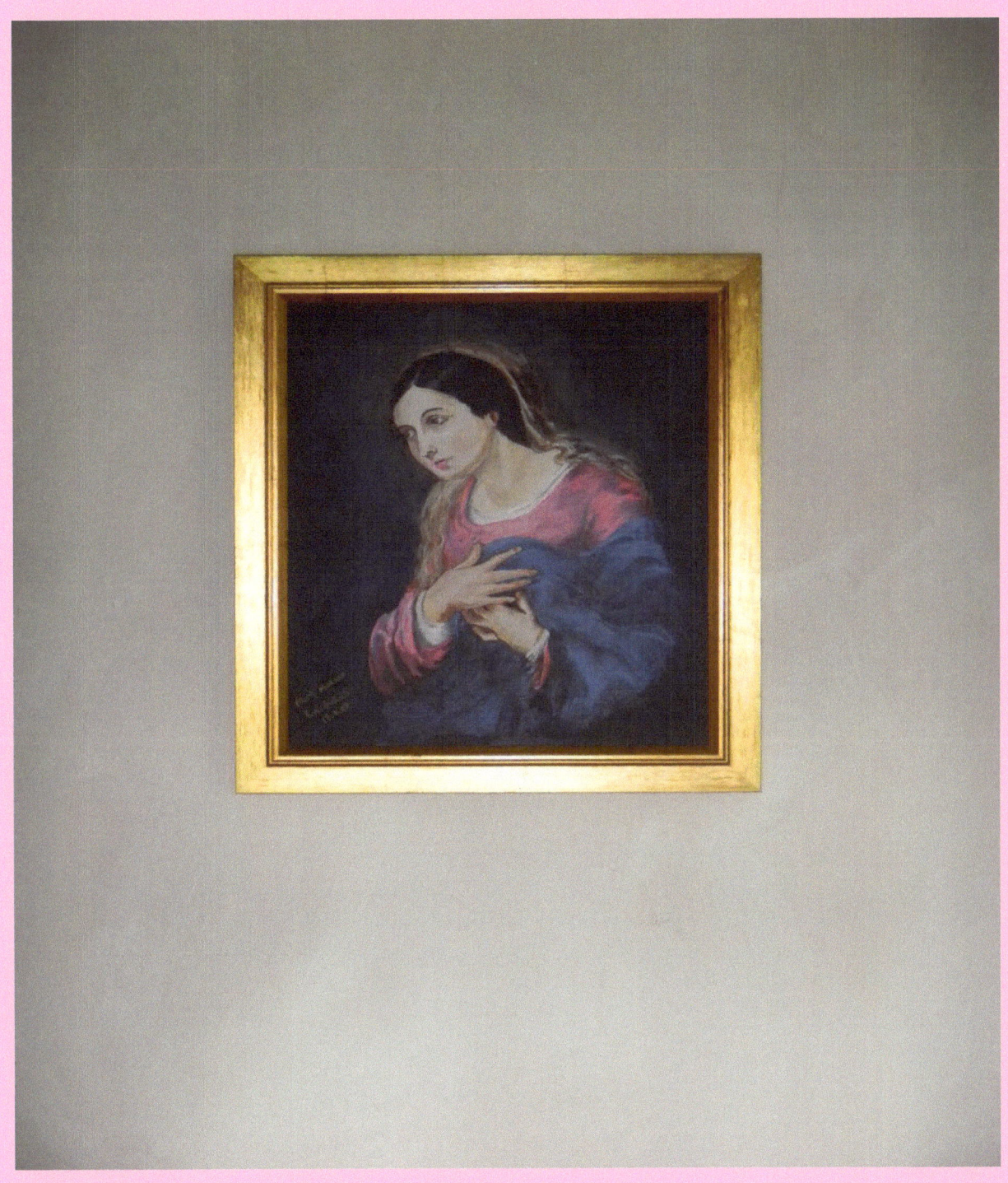

The painting on the left in the hallway is taken from Bartolomé Estaban Murillo's 'Annunciation'. Murillo (1617 - 1682) was a Spanish Baroque painter, best known for his religious works. He is often disparagingly referred to as 'Chocolate Box' by modern-day art historians, but no-one did tenderness like Murillo.

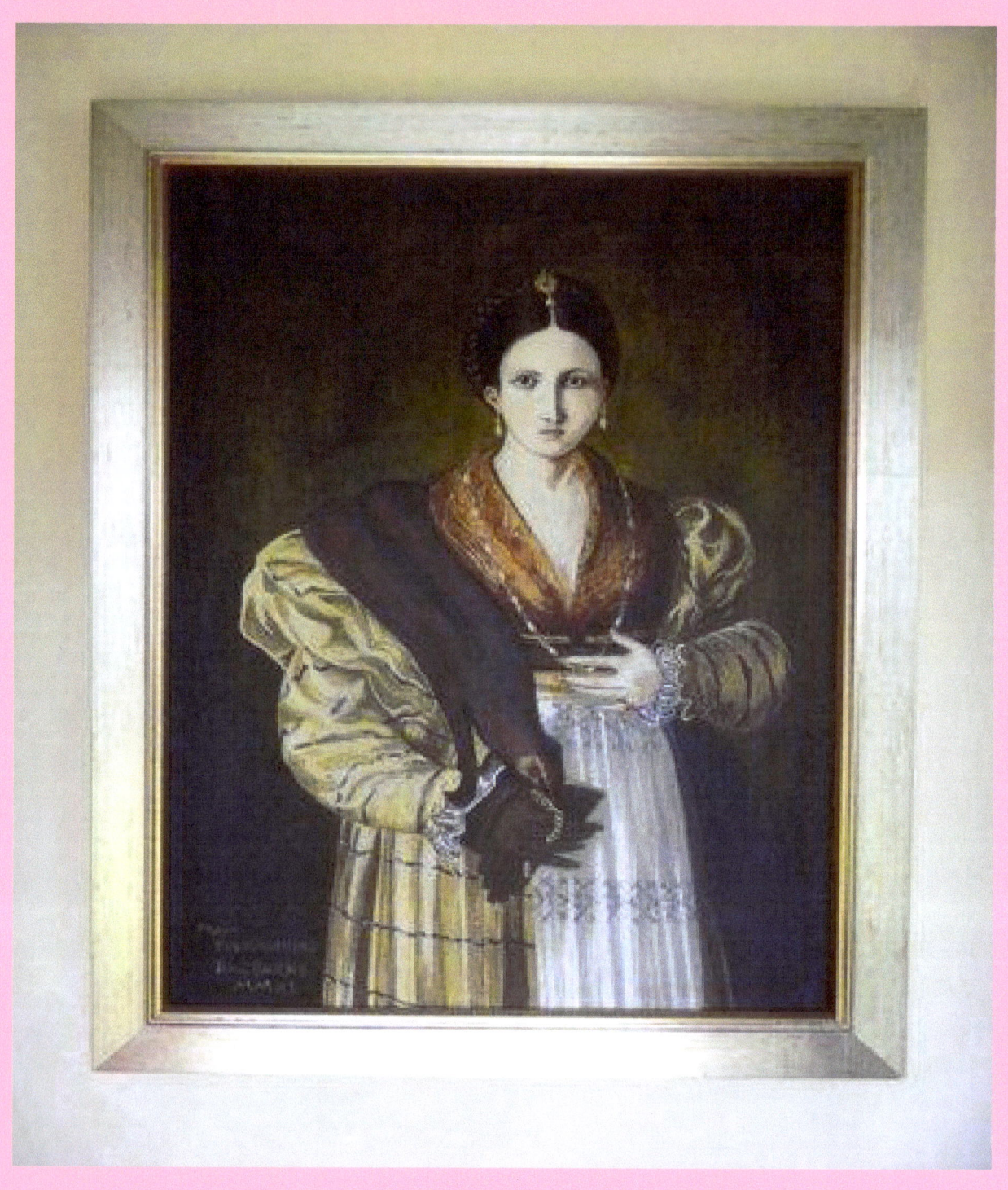

The painting on the right in the hallway is taken from Girolama Mazzola's 'Antea - Portrait of a Young Woman'. Mazzola (1503 - 1540) was commonly known as Parmigianino - 'the little one from Parma', and was best known for his elongated paintings. The garments depicted were considered luxurious in the 16th century.

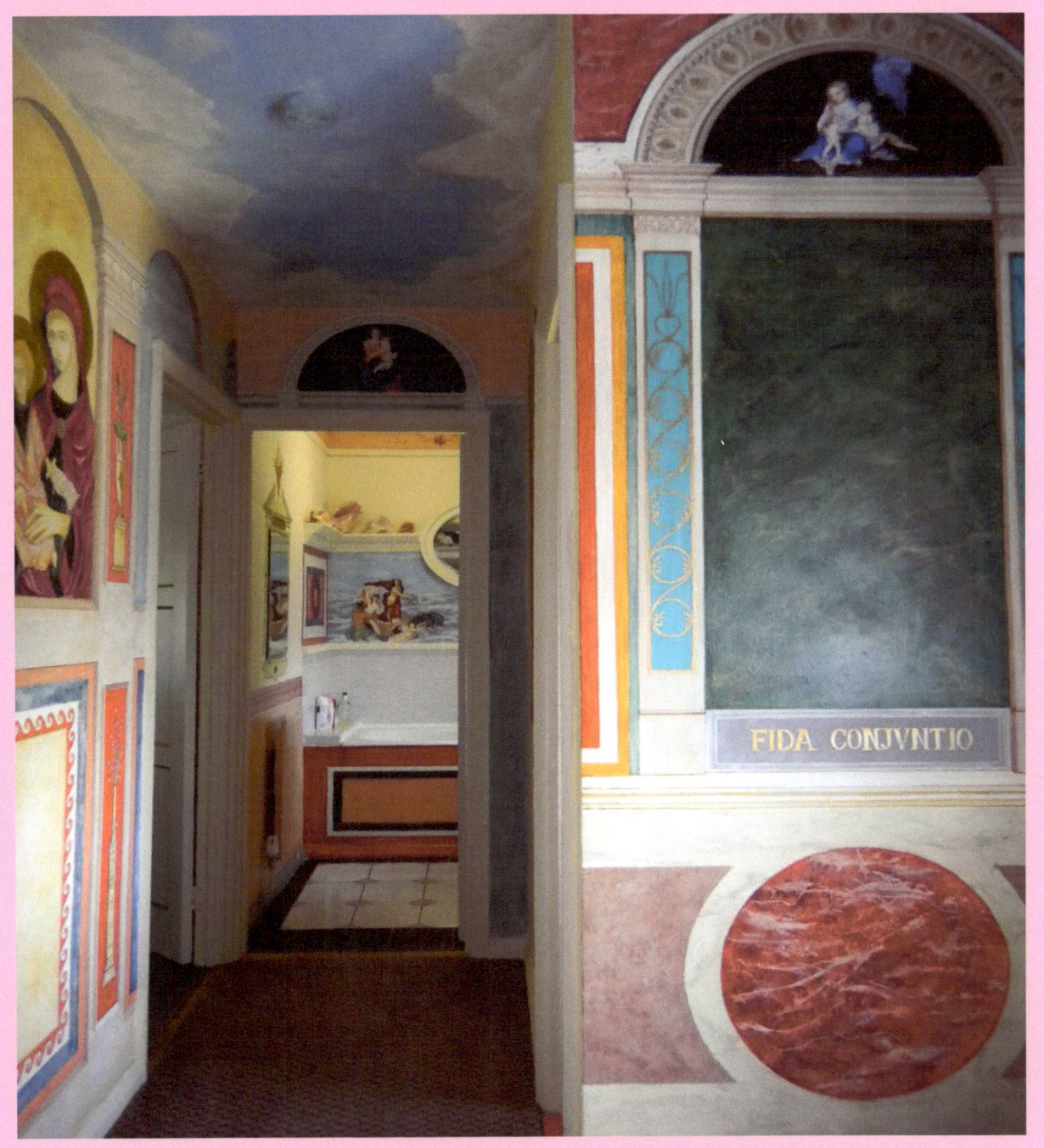

Passage to bathroom. The lunette above the rectangular faux marble on the right is taken from 'Madonna and Child with the Young Saint John' by Antonio da Correggio (1489 - 1534). The painting on the left-hand wall is taken from the circa 1500 Veneto-Cretan icon 'Madre Della Consolazione'. The lunette above the open bathroom door is taken from Murillo's 'Madonna and Child'.

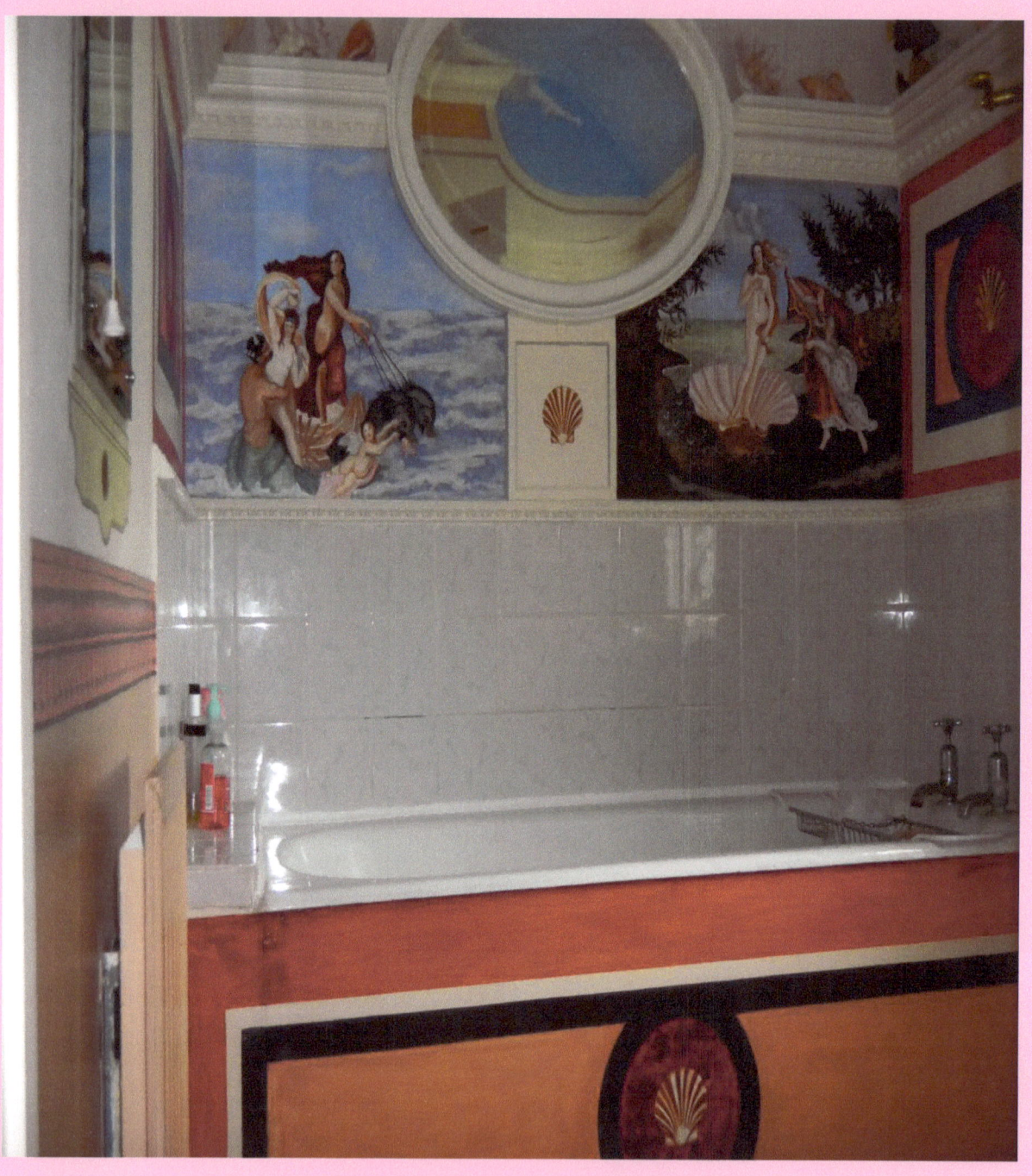

Bathroom. The painting on the left is taken from Raffaello Sanzio da Urbino's fresco masterpiece 'The Triumph of Galatea'. Urbino (1483 - 1520) was an Italian painter and architect, better known as 'Raphael'.

The painting on the right is taken from 'The Birth of Venus' by Sandro Botticelli (1445 - 1510).

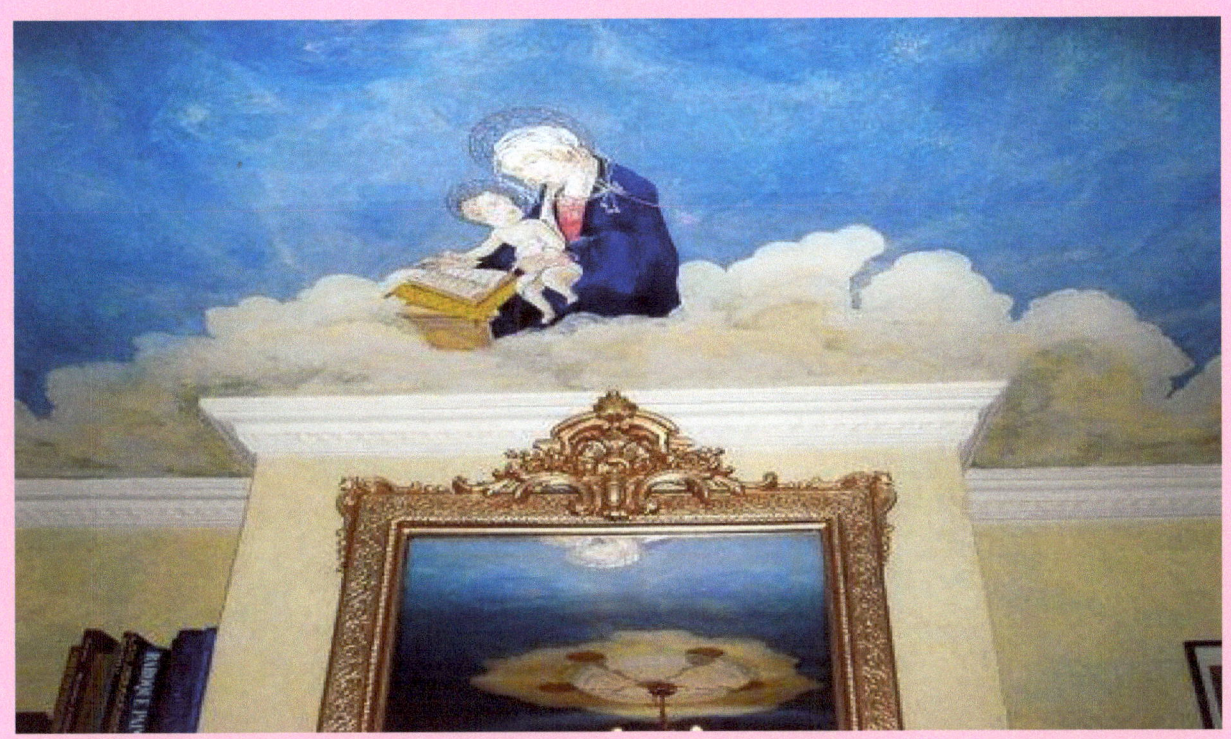

Lounge. The ceiling painting was taken from Botticelli's 'Madonna of the Book'. Many people believe that artists paint ceilings lying on their back, on a platform. Nothing could be further from the truth - the only way to paint ceilings is standing up, with your head tilted back.

The great Michelangelo di Lodovico Buonarotti Simoni (1475 - 1564) took four years to paint the ceiling of Rome's Sistine Chapel. His protégé and biographer Ascano Condivi once wrote "....having painted for so long a time, keeping his eyes fixed on the ceiling, he saw little when he looked down. If he had to read a letter or some other small thing, he was obliged to hold it above his head."

Michelangelo himself once wrote in poetry;

Defend my labour's cause,

good Giovanni, from all strictures:

I live in hell and paint its pictures.

7

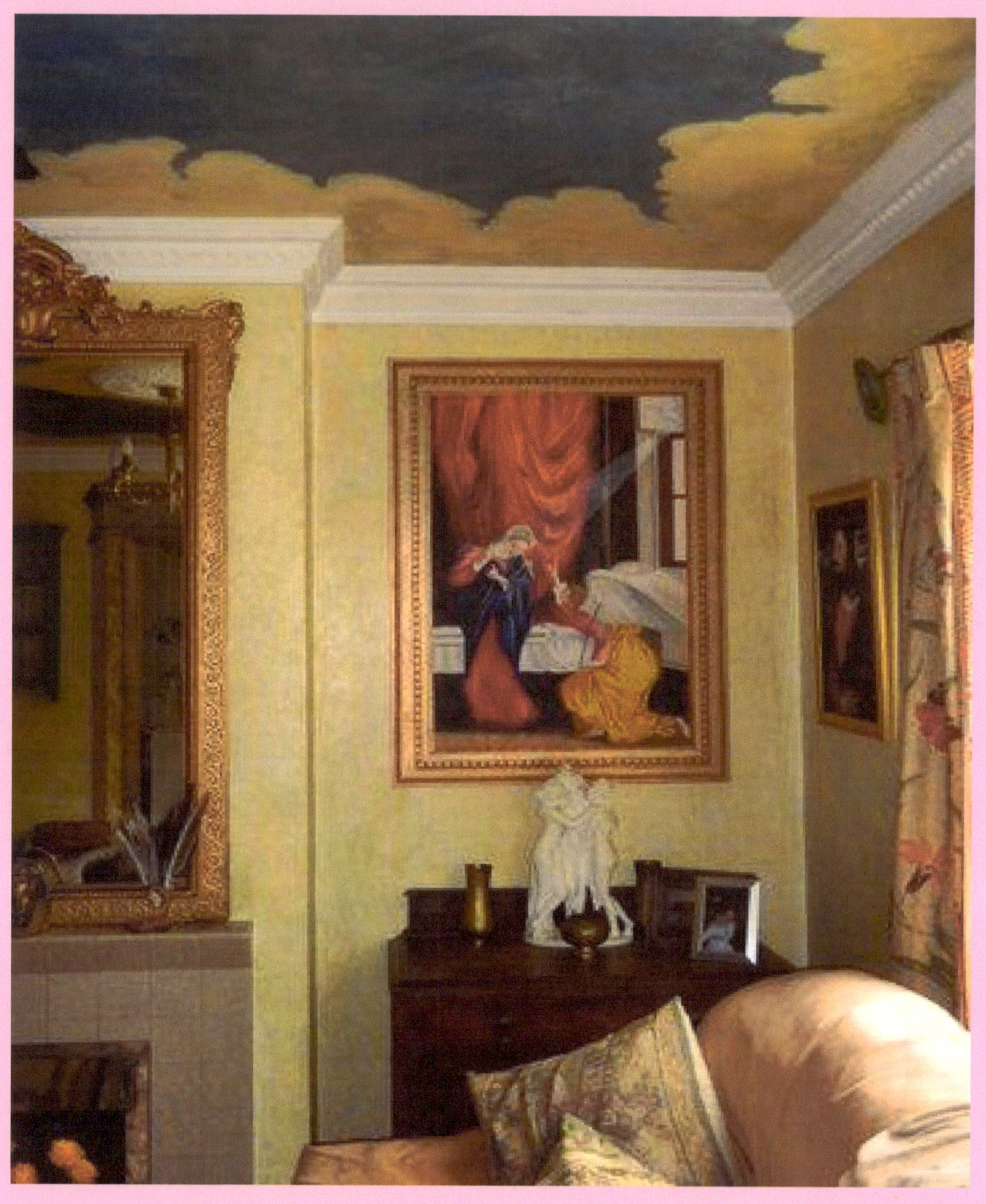

The portrait immediately to the right of the lounge mirror is taken from 'The Annunciation' by Orazio Lomi Gentileschi (1563 - 1639). I used a trompe-l'oeil frame, meaning the frame is painted on the wall.

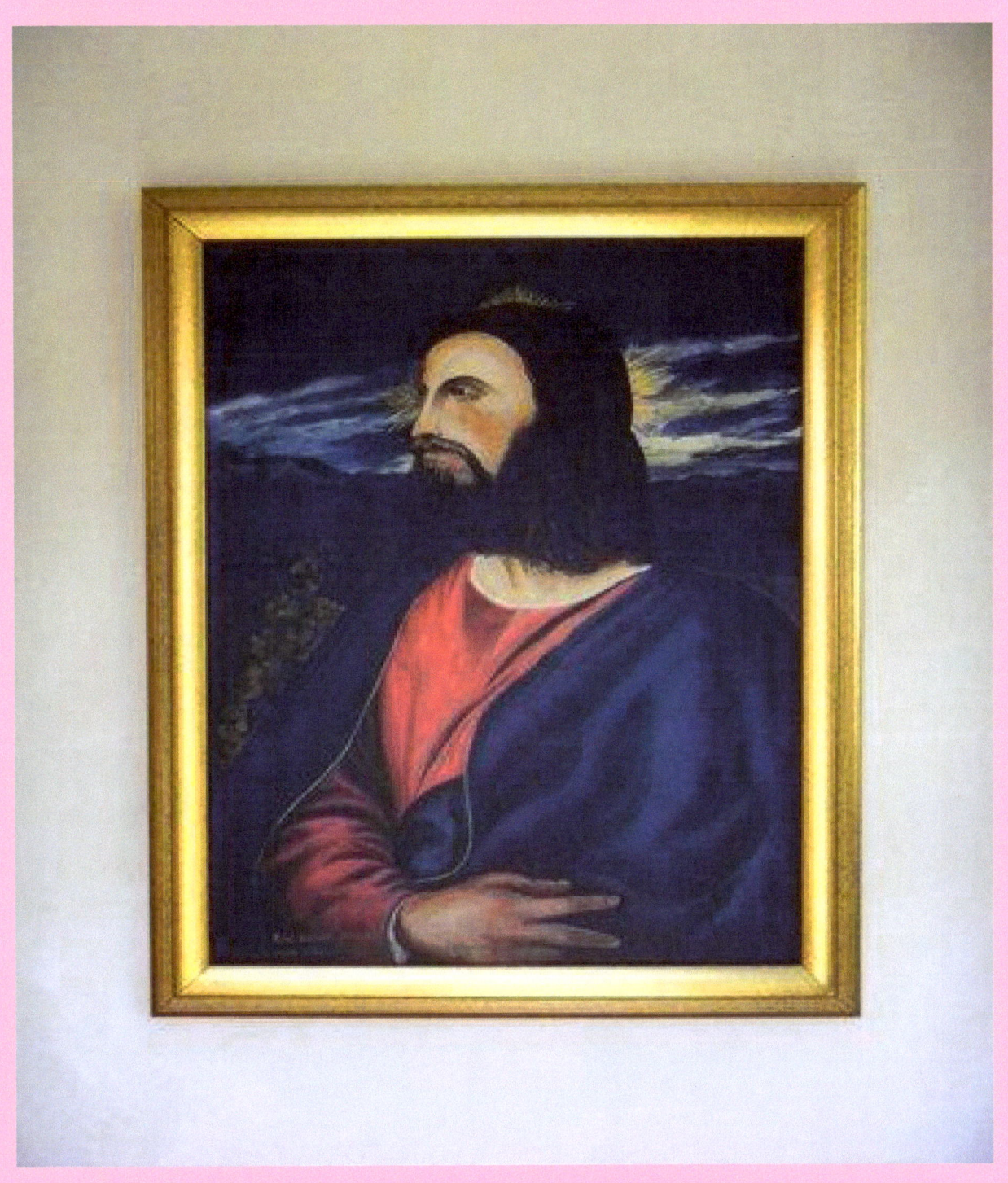

The portrait nearest the lounge curtain is taken from 'Christ the Redeemer' by Tiziano Vicelli. Vicelli (1488 - 1576) was more commonly known as 'Titian'. The extended thumb and fingers can be allegorically interpreted as representing the three Persons of the Holy Trinity.

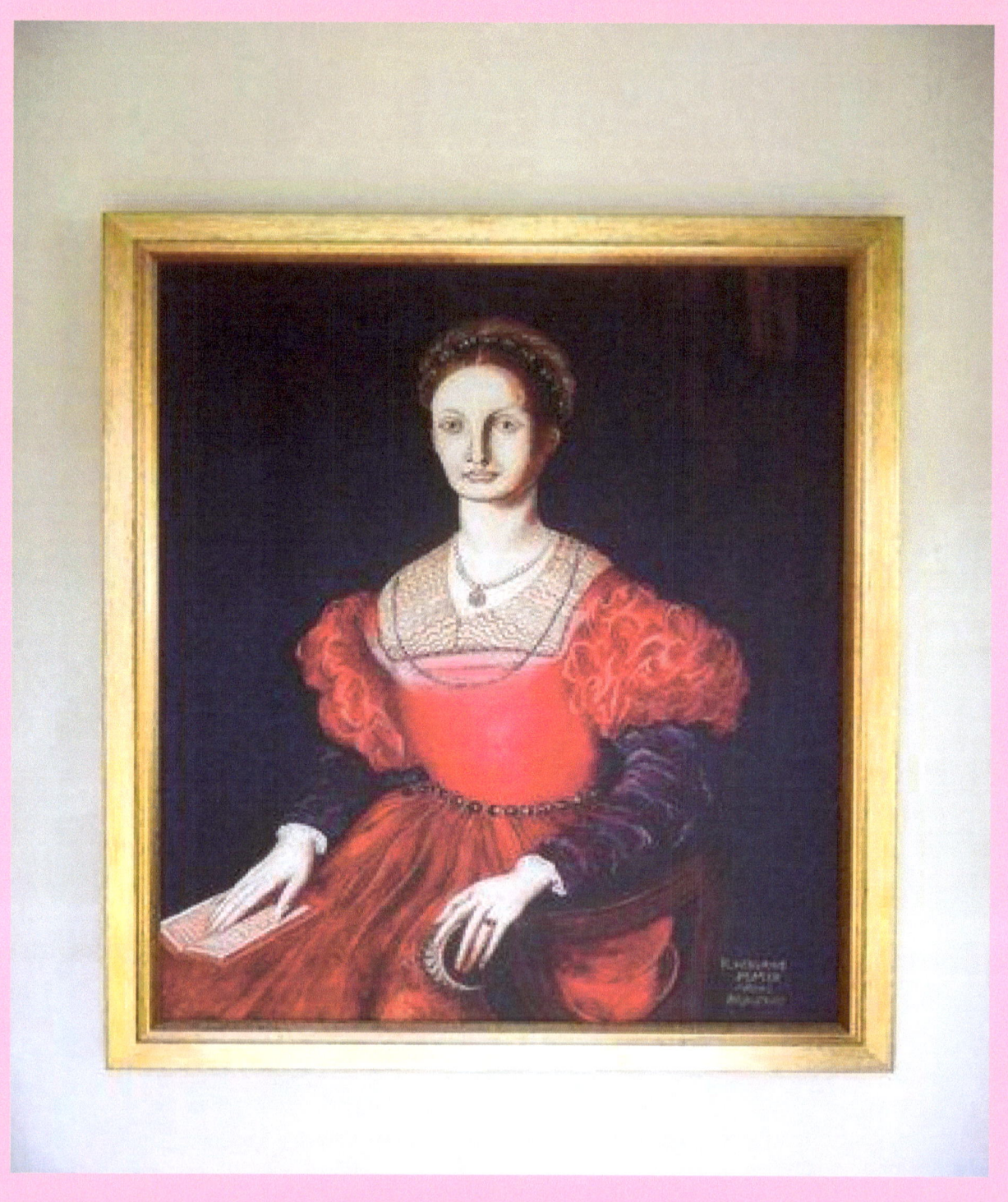

This portrait hanging in the lounge is taken from Agnolo di Cosimo's 'Portrait of Lucrezia Panciatichi'. Cosimo (1503 - 1572) was commonly known as 'Bronzino', which in all probability referred to his skin tone. Bronzino was the finest of the Renaissance portrait painters.

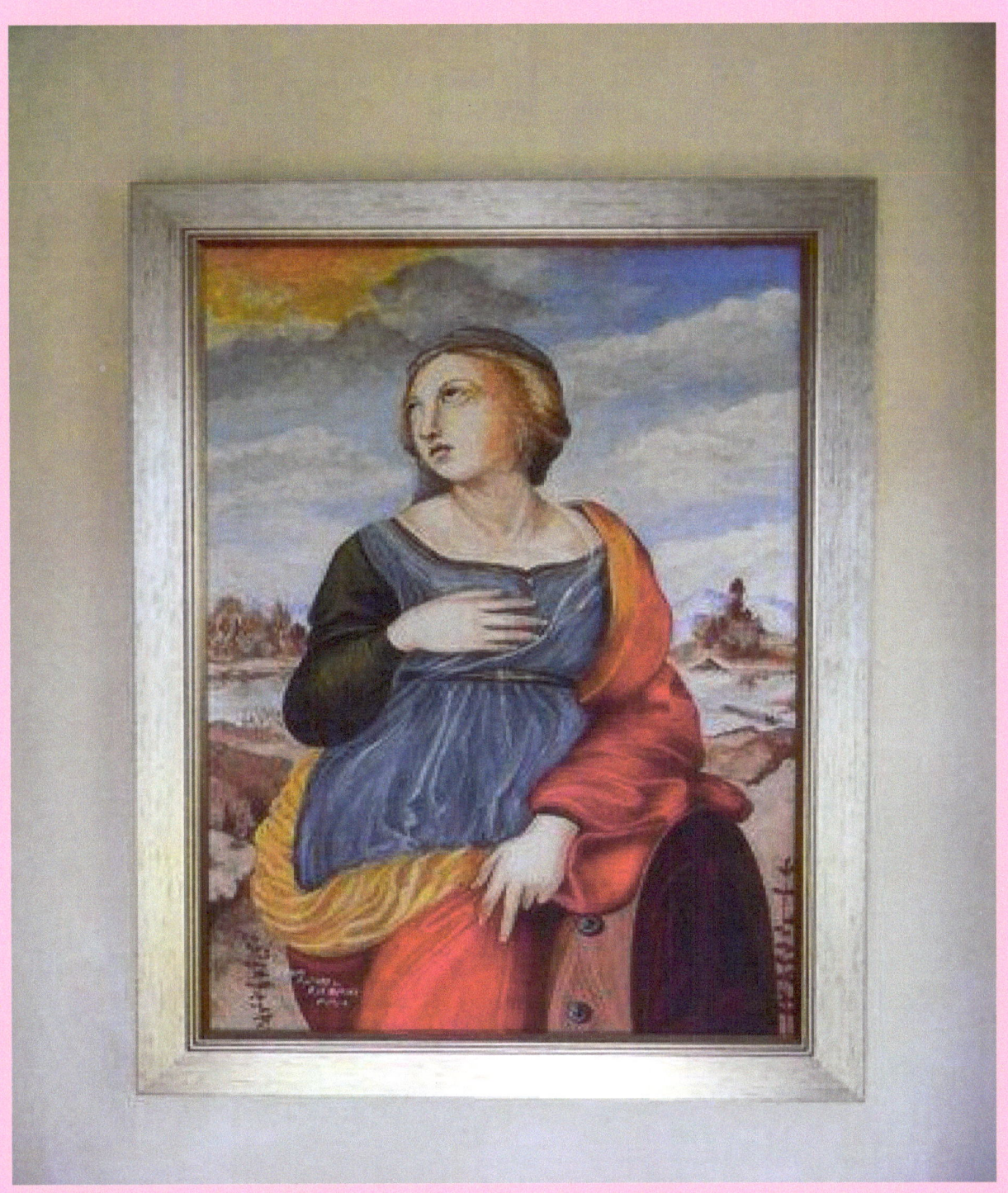

Also hanging in the lounge, this portrait is taken from Raphael's 'Saint Catherine of Alexandria'. Catherine is shown leaning on a wheel, which is common in depictions of her, because according to legend, she was martyred on a wheel. The legend provides the name for the modern-day Catherine wheel firework.

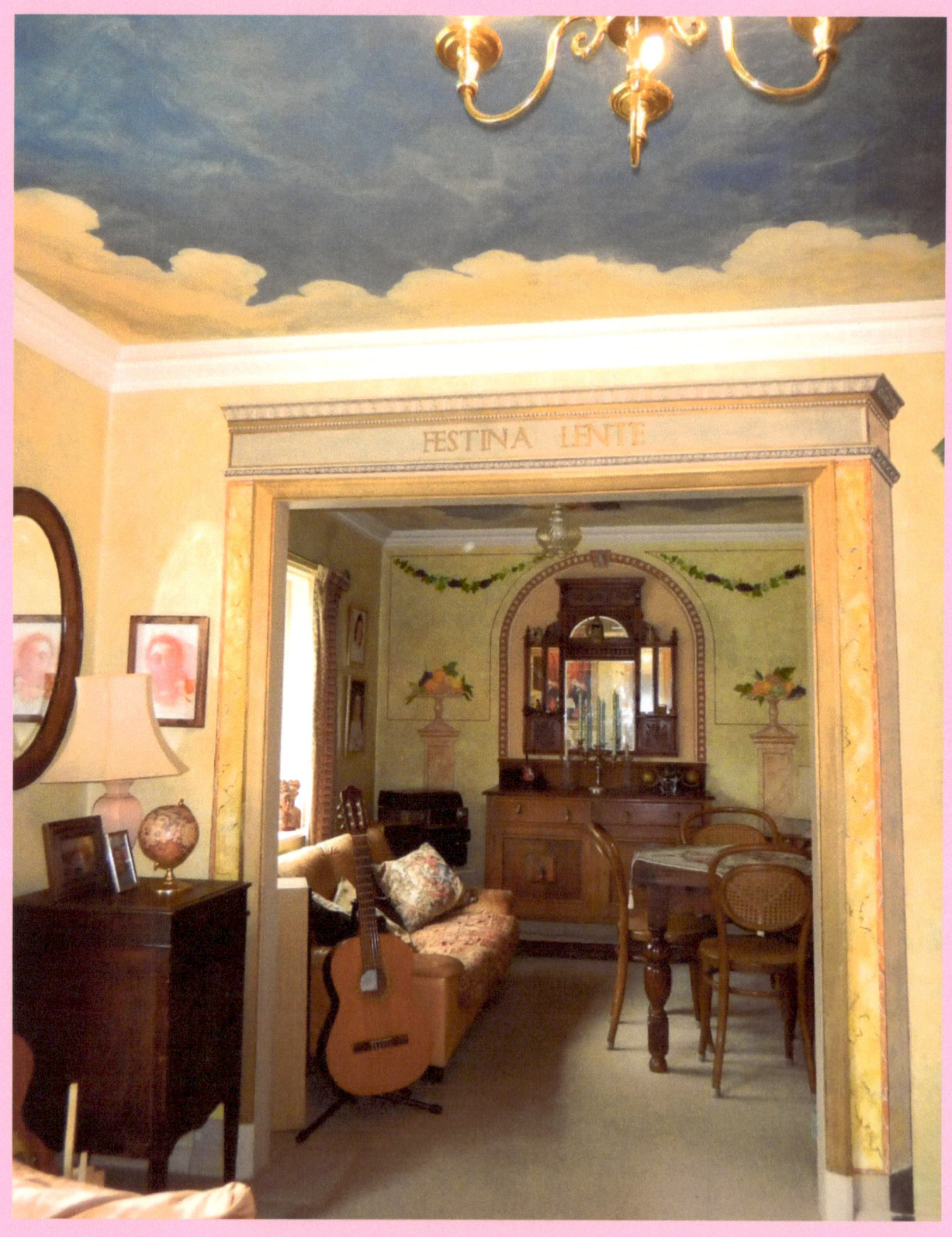

View from lounge to dining room. The Latin inscription on the arch means 'hasten slowly', i.e. have caution with energy.

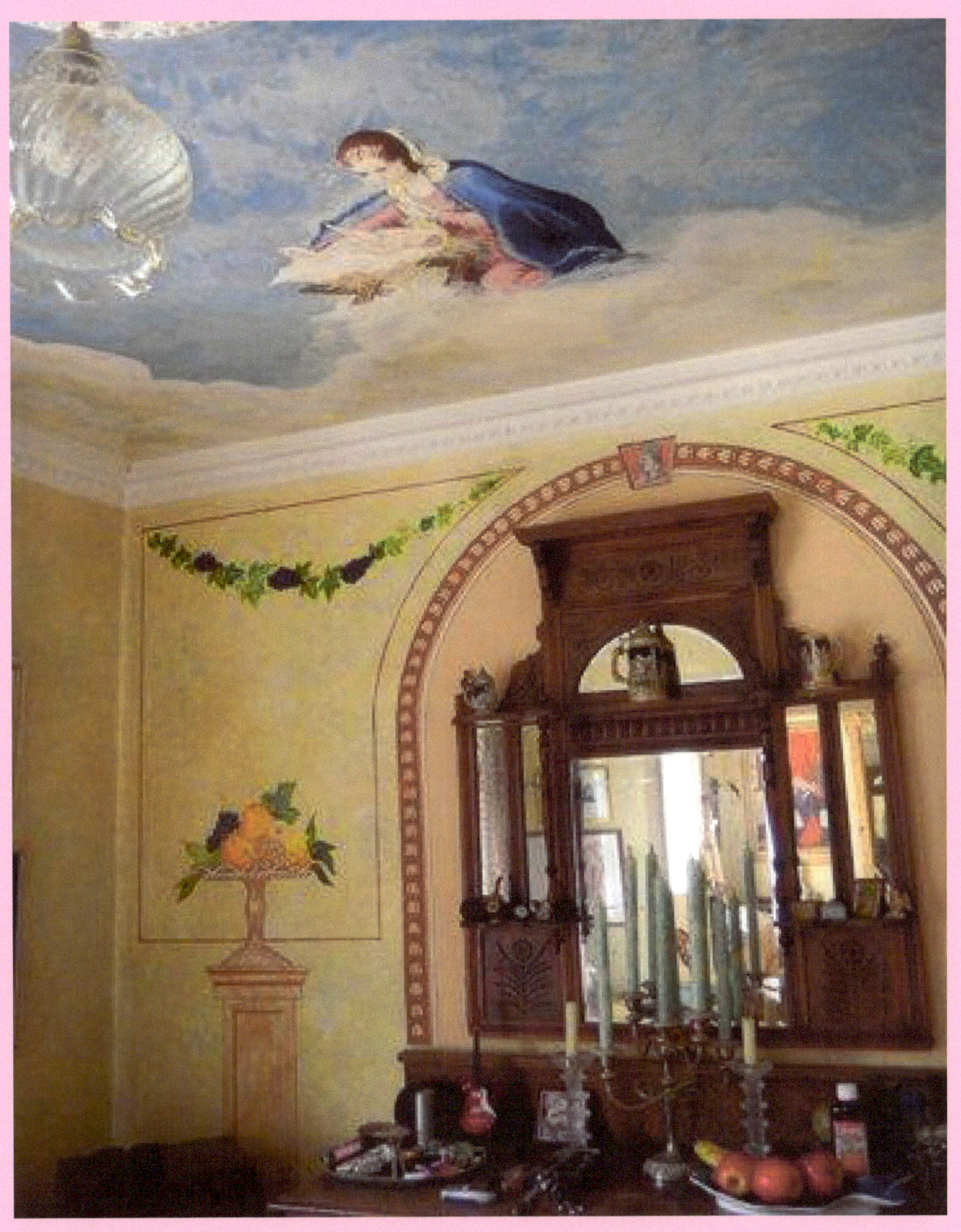

Dining room. The ceiling detail is taken from 'The Nativity' by Giambattista Pittoni (1687 - 1767). This was my first ceiling painting.

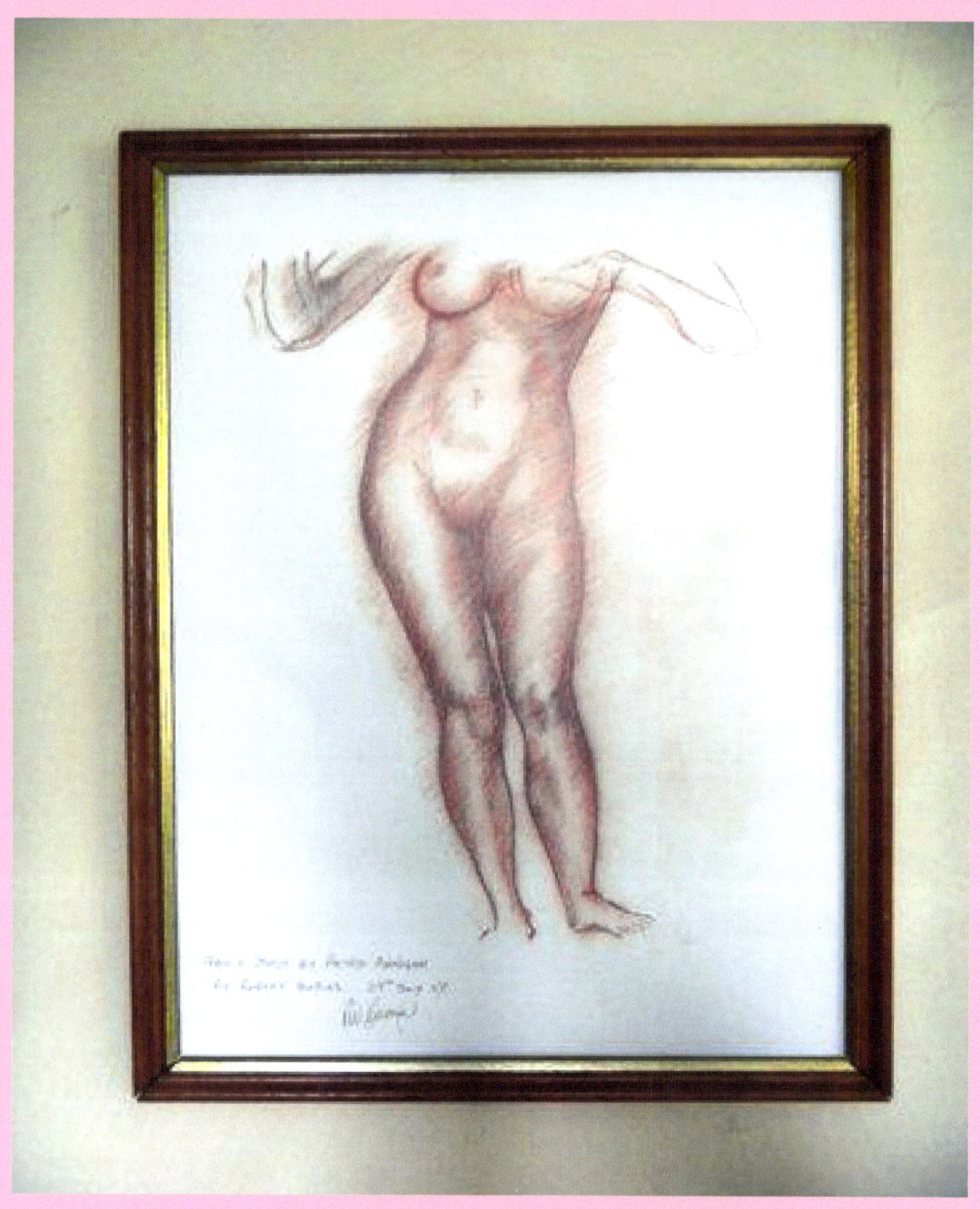

Just visible in the dining room mirror is this reproduction of a study by Pietro Annigoni (1910 - 1988). Annigoni became famous for his portrait of Queen Elizabeth II in 1956. I was commissioned to produce this reproduction using terracotta chalks.

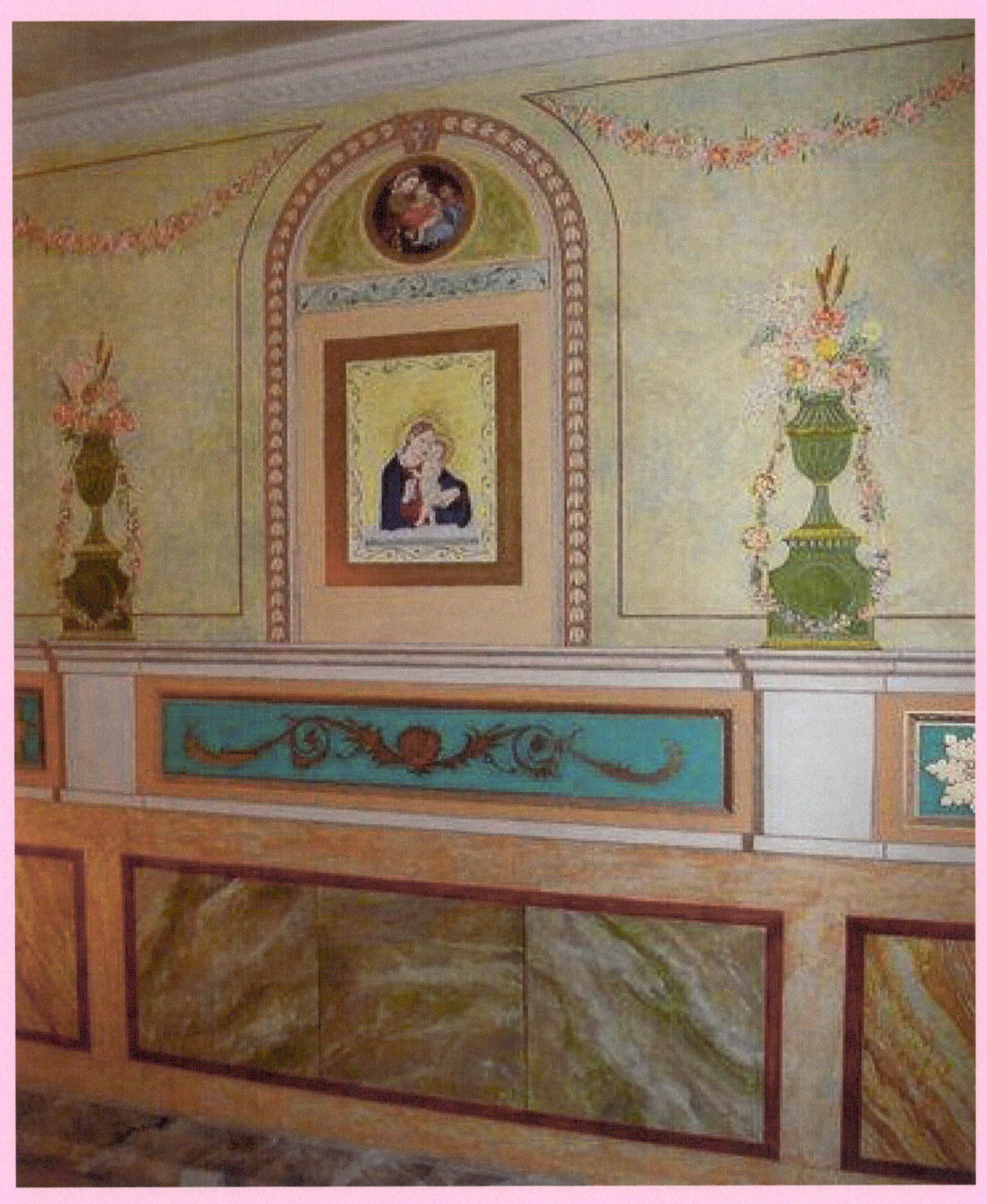

The circular picture in the dining room is taken from Raphael's 'Madonna of the Chair'.

The lowermost picture is based on 'Madonna and Child with Two Cherubim' by Antoniazzo Romano (1430 - 1510).

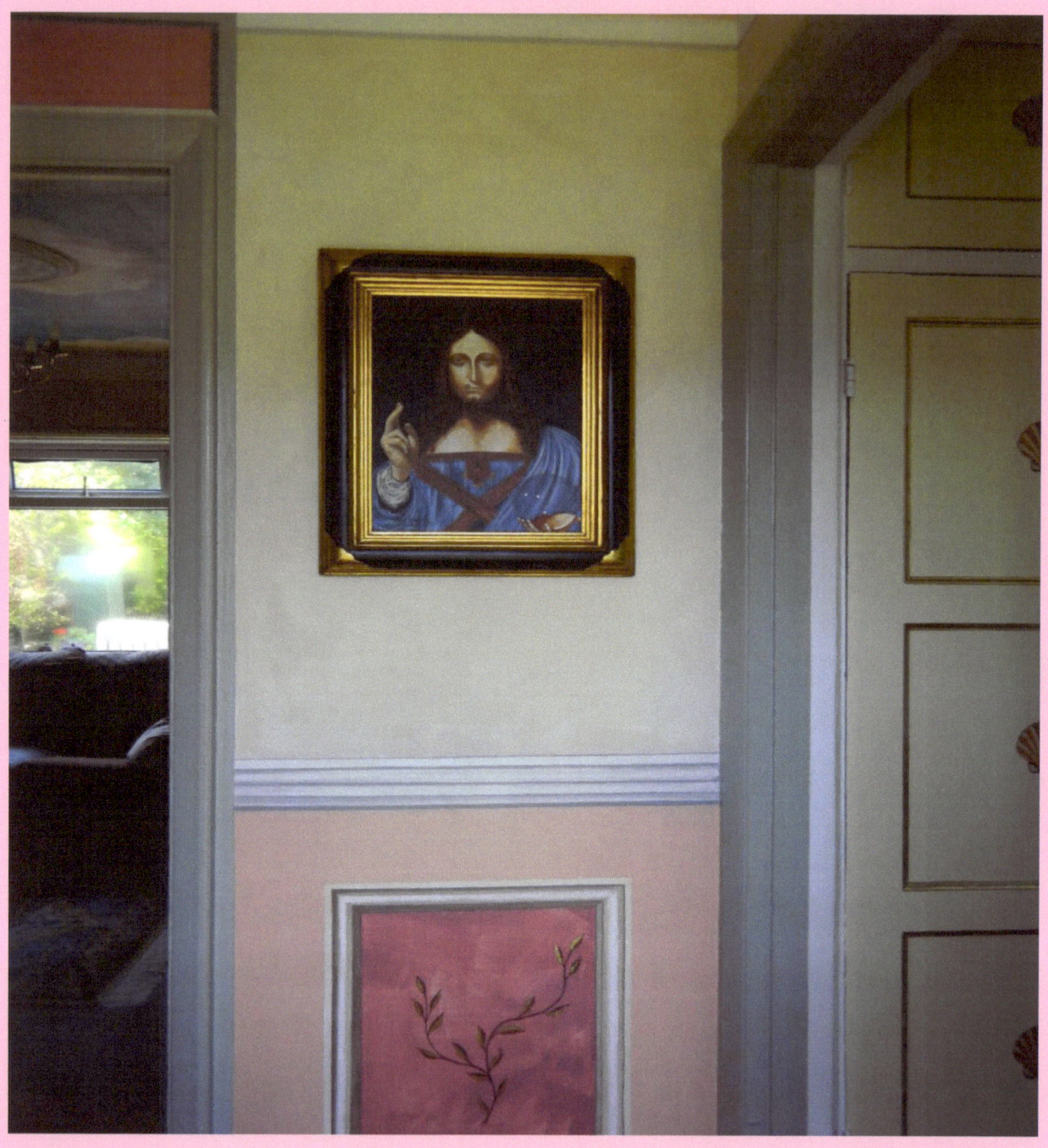

Hall. This portrait is taken from Leonardo Da Vinci's long-lost 'Salavator Mundi' - saviour of the world. Owned by Charles I and Charles II, the original remained in London for 500 years, before becoming lost in the mid-20th century. Rediscovered and attributed to Da Vinci in 2011, his depiction of Christ is worth a world record £120m. Christ's outstretched hand almost seems to come out of the canvas.

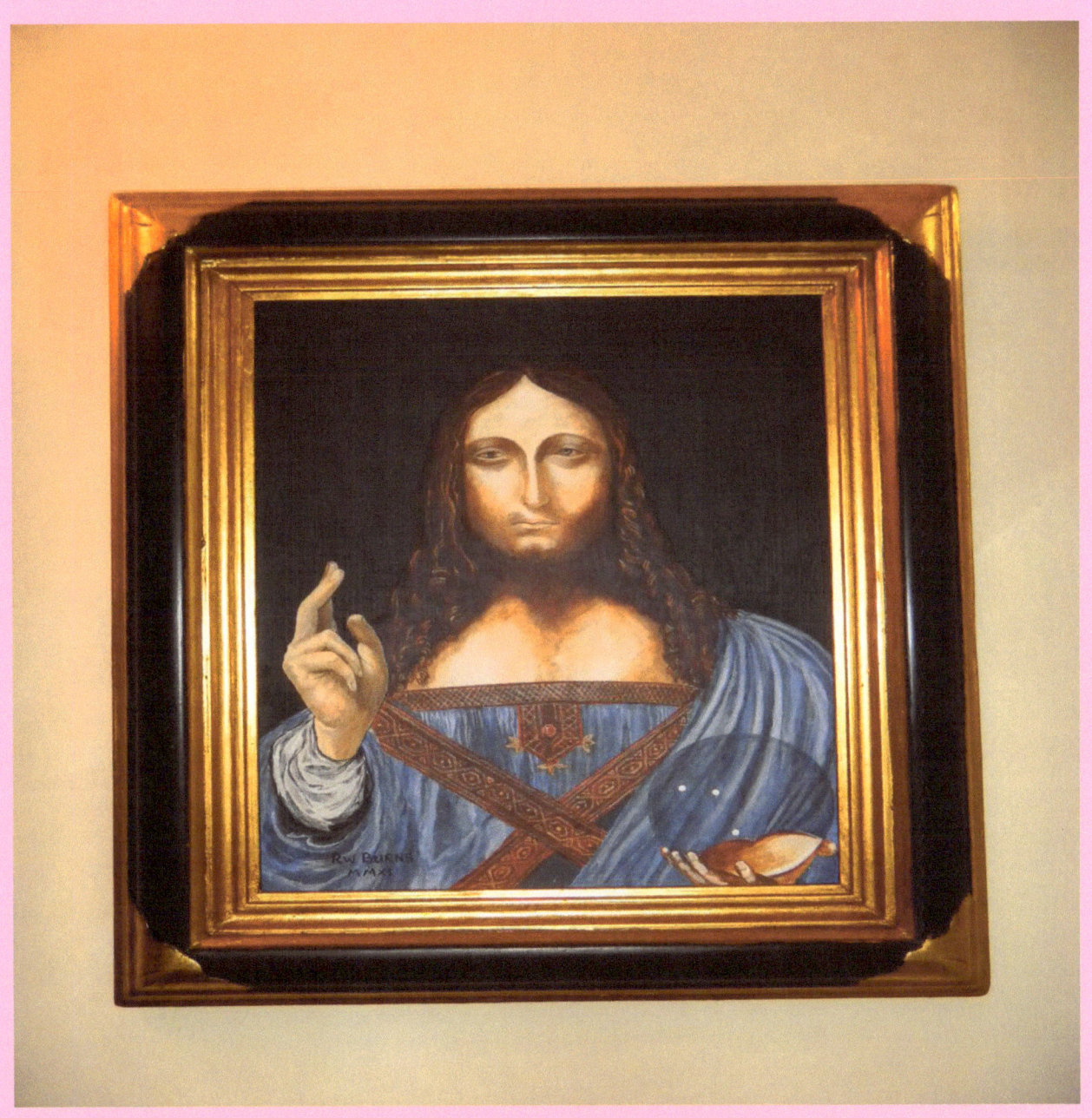

Da Vinci (1452 - 1519) was renowned primarily as a painter, one of the greatest of all time, most famously for 'Mona Lisa'. But his genius extended to sculpture, architecture, science, mathematics, engineering, anatomy, geology, cartography, botany and writing, and as such, he was perhaps the most diversely talented genius ever to have lived. Technologically ingenious, he conceptualised a helicopter, a tank, solar power, a calculator and a double hull.

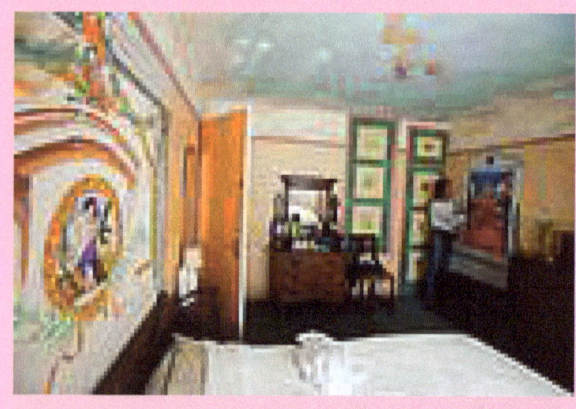

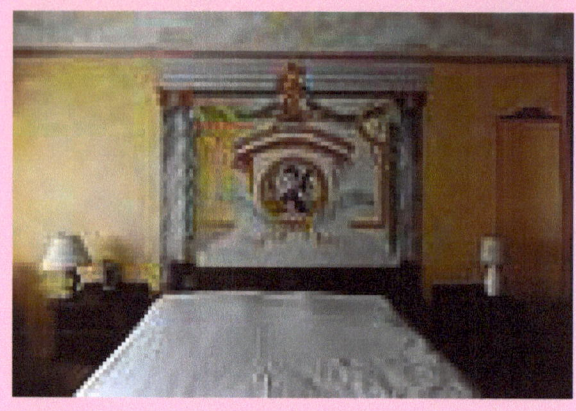

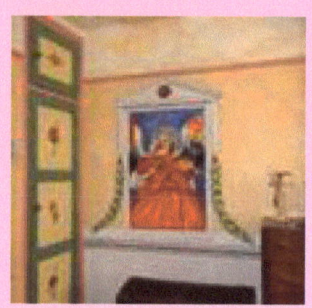

Studio room. The picture over the bed is taken from a mural copy of 'Cupid Disarmed' by academic painter Guillaume Seignac (1870 - 1924), on display at a house in Rome.

The portrait on the right is taken from 'Musician Angel' by Melozzo da Forli (1438 - 1494), who was known for his foreshortening painting technique. da Forli's original was destroyed in 1711, but 14 fragments are on display at the Vatican.

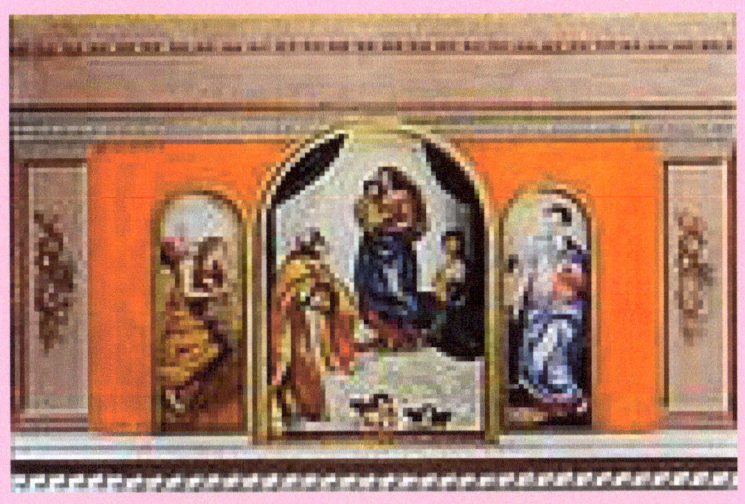

This triptych also appears in the studio room. The side panel figures are taken from works of Bronzino, which currently flank his 'Disposition of Christ' at the Palazzo Vecchio, Florence.

The central panel is taken from Raphael's enigmatic 'Sistine Madonna', the finest painting of the Renaissance. The original was commissioned in the 16th century by the Monastery of San Sisto in Piacenza, where it was used an altarpiece. Its troubled history saw it move to Dresden in 1754, before being stored in a tunnel to escape bombing in World War II. Seized by the Red Army at the end of the war, it was transported by train to Moscow, before being returned to Dresden in 1955.

'Sistine' does not relate to Rome's Sistine Chapel. Madonna and child are flanked by Saint Barbara and Pope Sixtus II, the latter of which commissioned the Sistine Chapel in the 15th century.

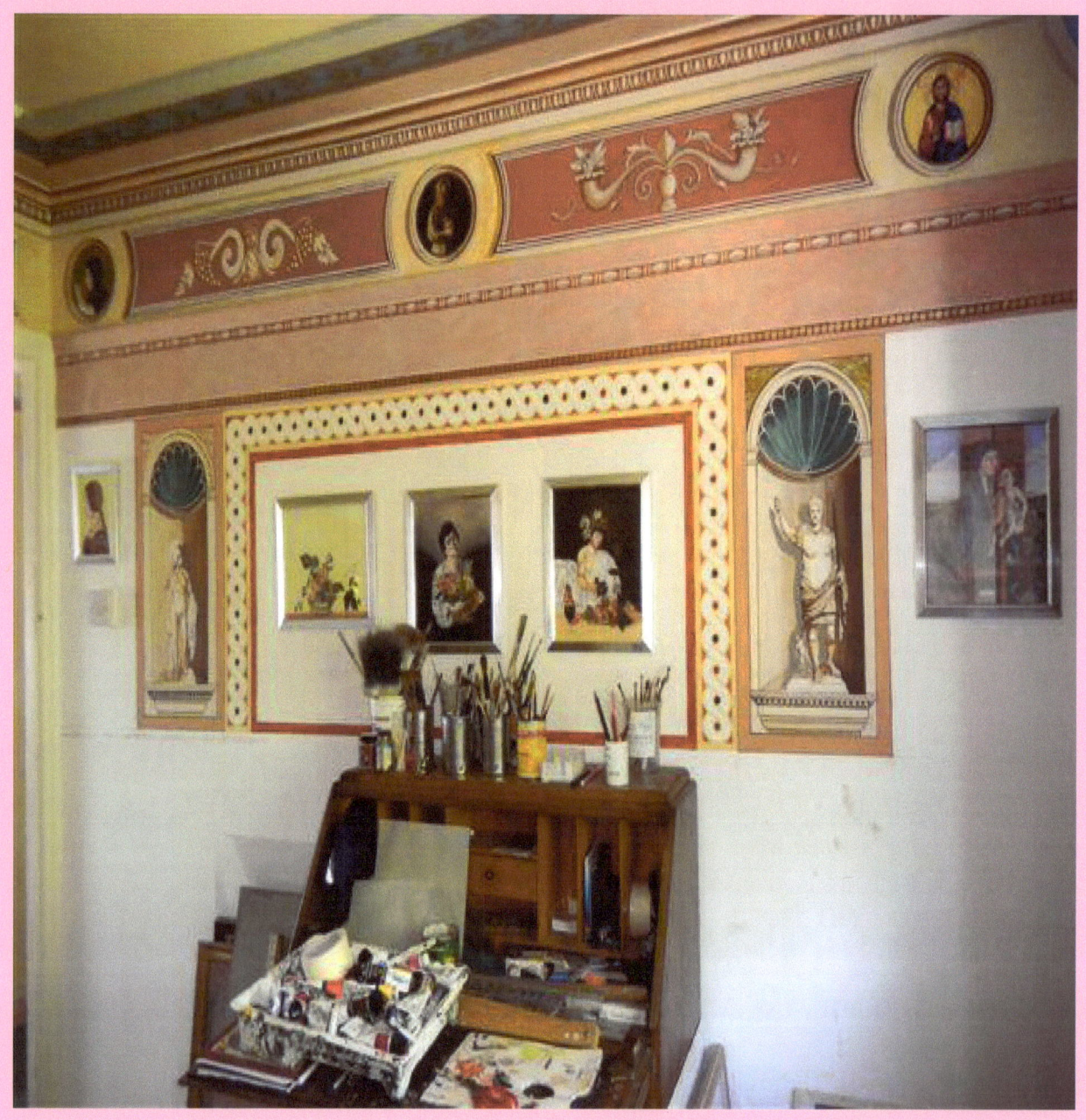

The studio room includes many other detailed Renaissance-style panels, set around portraits. The three portraits in the central panel are all taken from works of Michelangelo Merisi da Caravaggio (1571 -1610).

The portrait towards the left of the panel is taken from 'Basket of Fruit'. The central portrait is taken from 'Boy with a Basket of Fruit'. The portrait at the right of the panel is taken from 'Bacchus'.

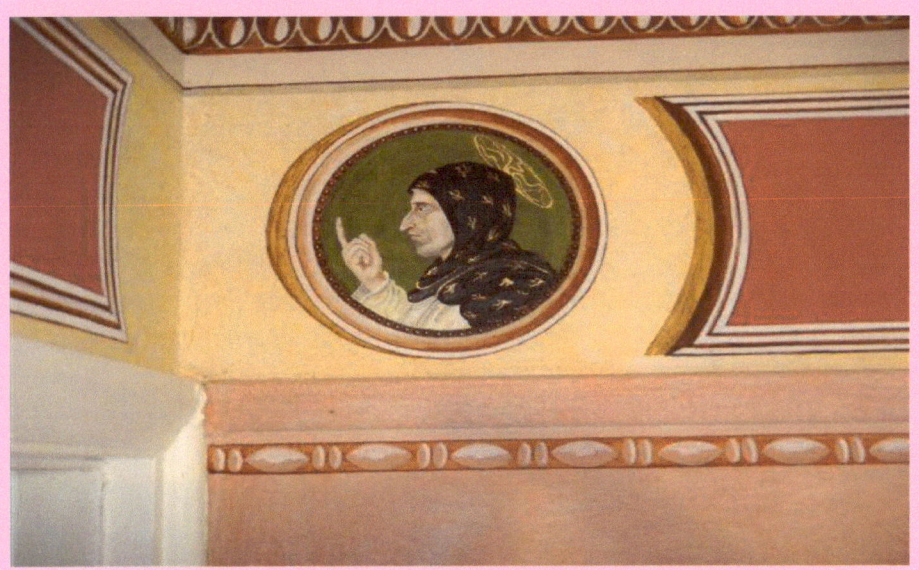

This picture is taken from a portrait of Girolamo Savonarola by Dominican nun Polyxena de Nelli (1523 - 1588). Polyxena was also known by the name Suor Plautilla Nelli.

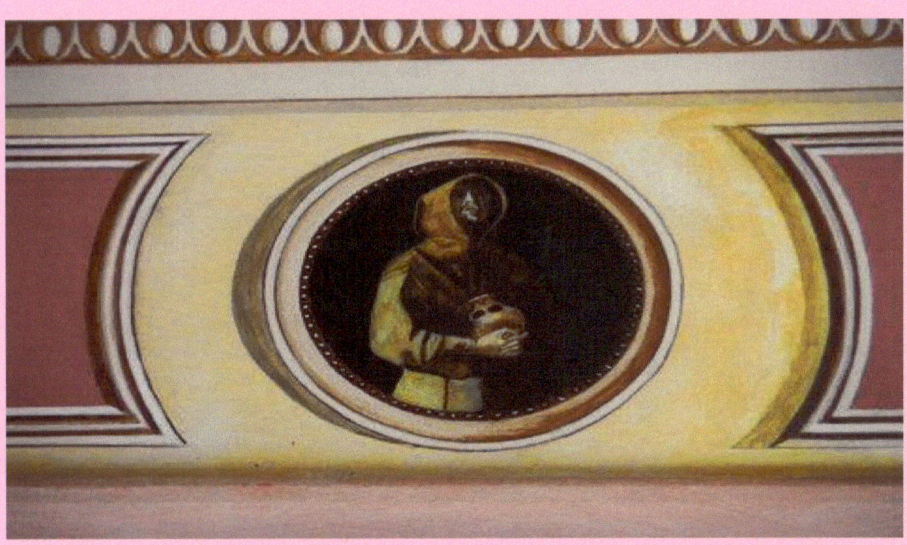

This picture is taken from 'Saint Francis in Meditation' by Francisco de Zurbaran. Zurbaran (1598 - 1664) was known for his paintings of monks, nuns, martyrs and still-life. He died in poverty and obscurity, after his hard-edged works were unfavourably compared with those of Murillo.

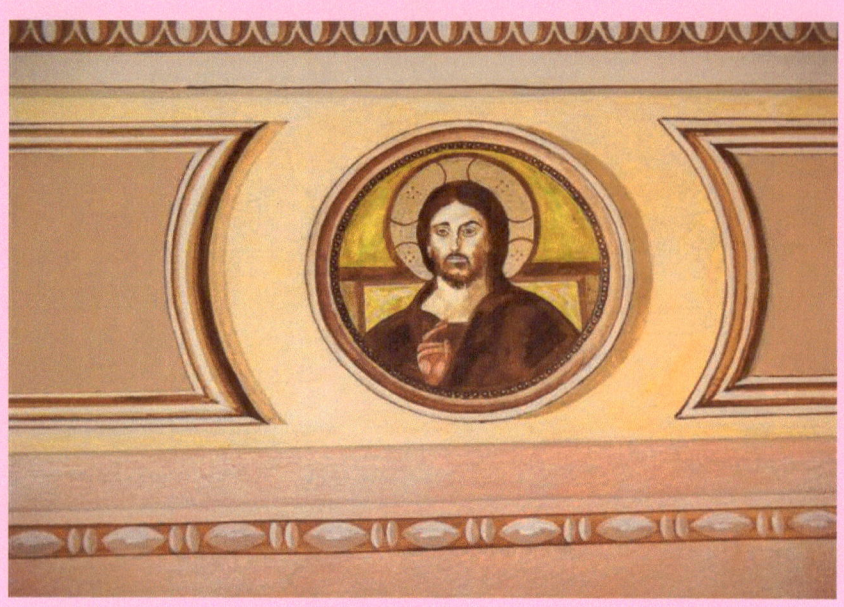

This picture is based on 'Christ Pantocrator', the oldest known icon of Christ. The icon is held at St. Catherine's Monastery, Mount Sanai, and dates from the 6th, or possibly even 5th century.

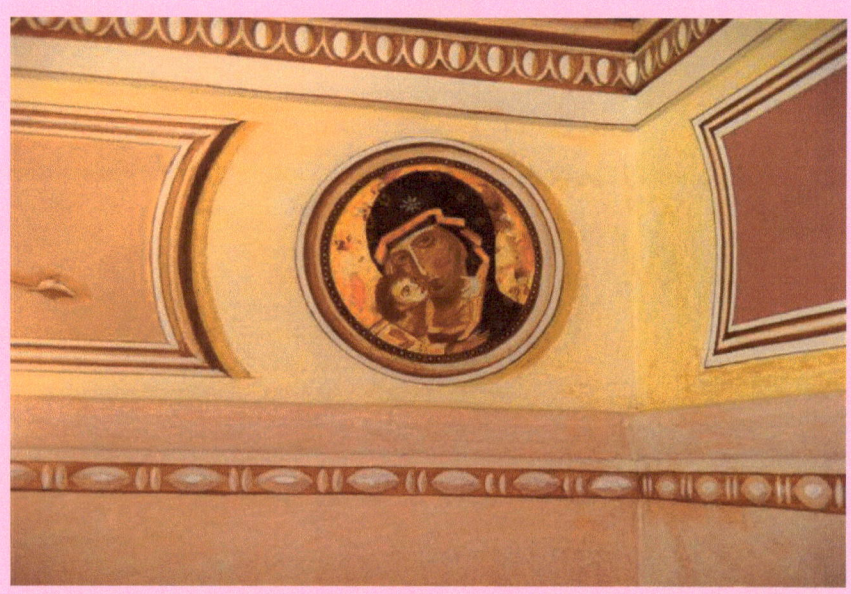

This picture is based on the venerated Orthodox Church icon 'Our Lady of Vladimir', which dates back to 1131.

There are many other paintings dotted around the house, including;

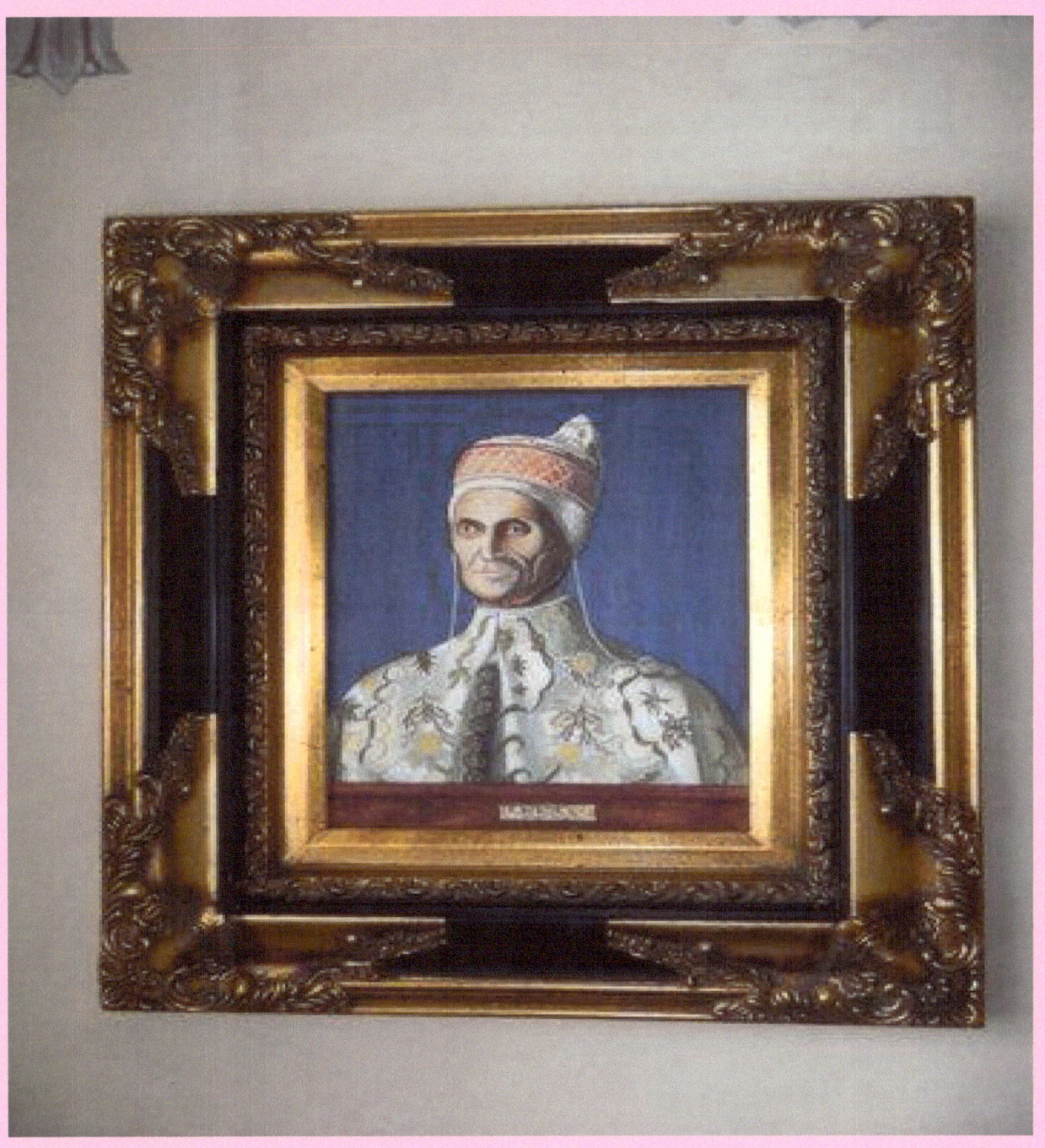

This painting is taken from 'Portrait of Doge Leonardo Loredan' by Giovanni Bellini (1430 - 1516). At 8 x 10 inches, my portrait is much smaller than the original, but looks great in this antique frame.

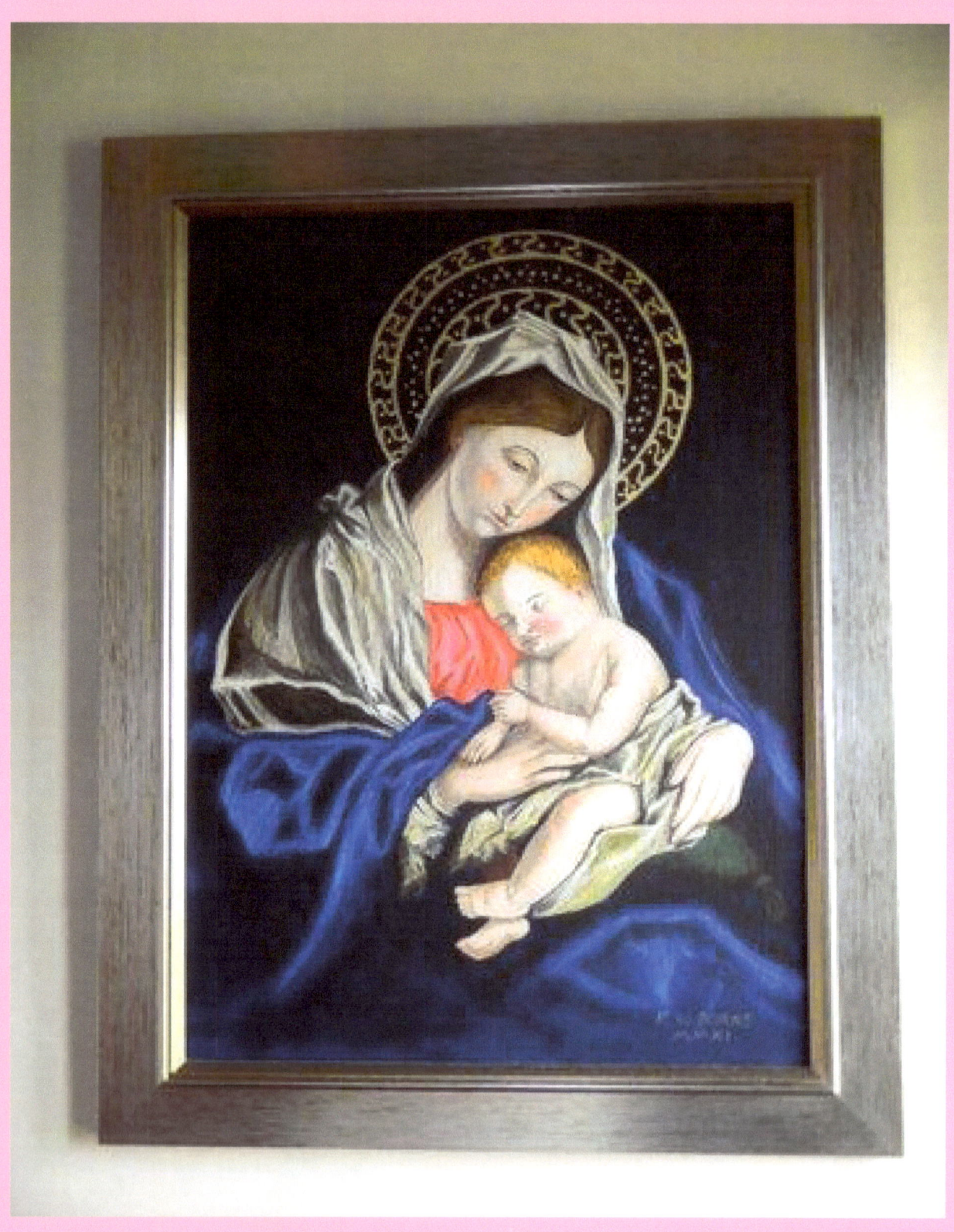

This portrait is based on 'Madonna and Child' by Baroque painter Giovanni Battista Salvi (1609 - 1685). The tenderness Salvi captured between mother and child is astonishing.

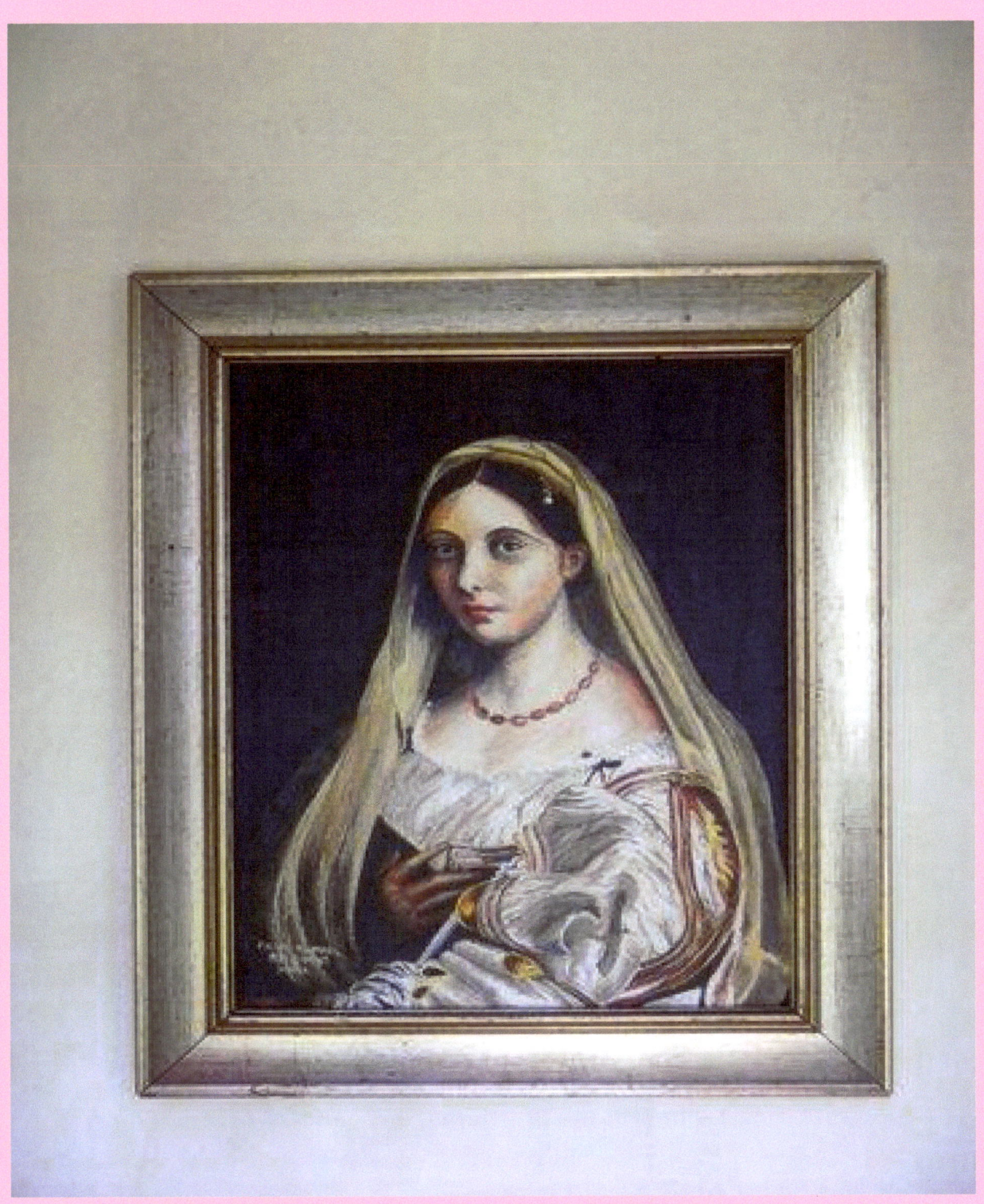

This portrait is taken from Raphael's 'Woman in a Veil'. The subject is Margherita Luti, Raphael's Roman mistress. Margherita also appeared in Raphael's 'La Fornarina' - the baker's daughter.

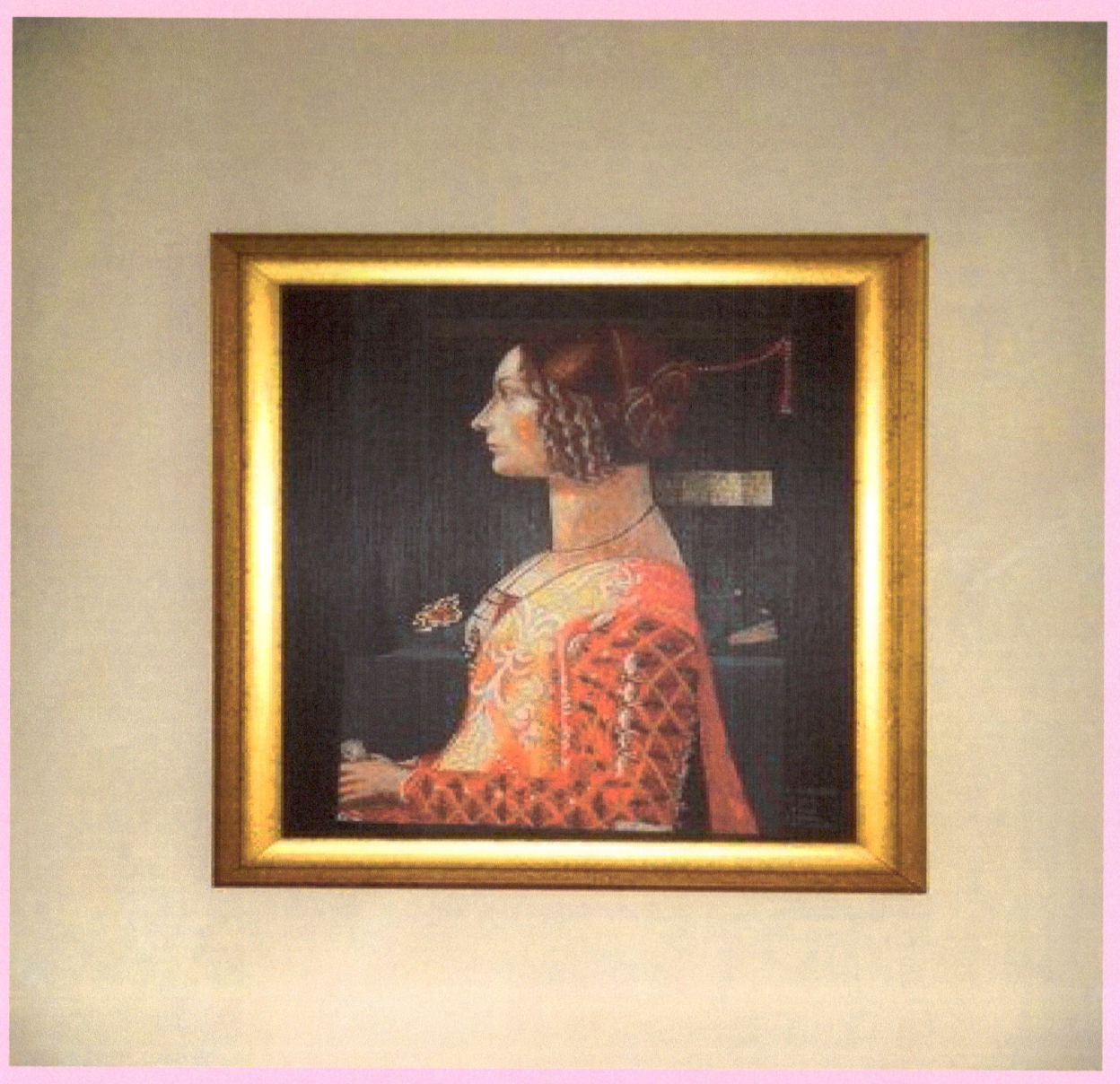

This painting is taken from 'Portrait of Giovanna Tornabuoni' by Domenico Ghirlandaio (1449 - 1494). Michelangelo di Lodovico Buonarotti Simoni was once an apprentice of Ghirlandaio.

Ghirlandaio completed the original in 1488, the same year Tornabuoni died in childbirth. Tornabuoni's death probably preceded the original, hence the feeling of sadness conveyed in the pose. Above the prayer book on a shelf behind the subject, the hanging red coral necklace is probably a rosary.

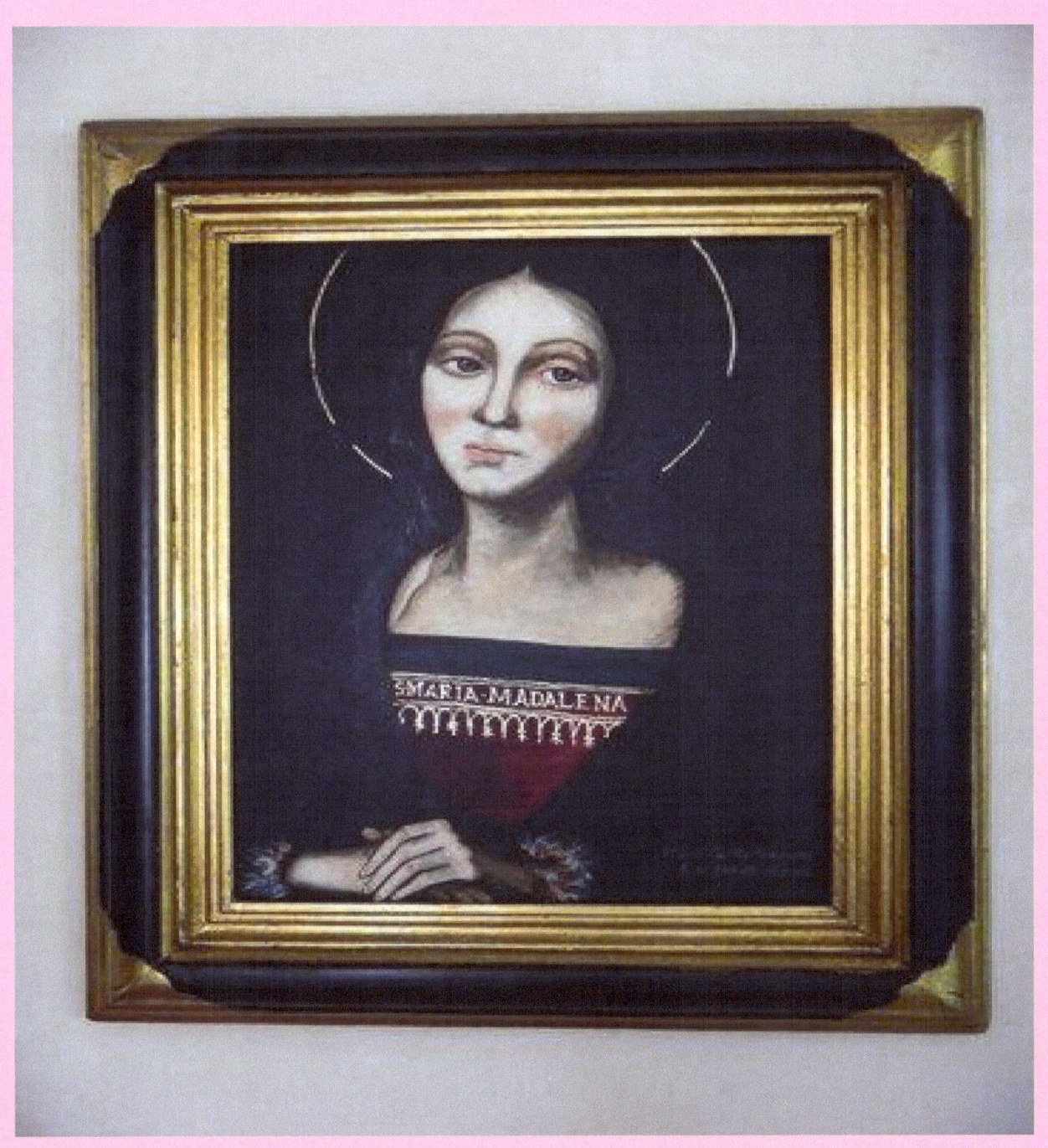

This portrait is taken from 'St. Mary Magdalene' by Pietro Perugino (1450 - 1523). Raphael was a pupil of Perugino. For many years, the original was falsely attributed to Leonardo Da Vinci, because of the quality of the near-monochrome palette, and the melancholy look of the eyes. Another striking feature of the original was its subtle use of gold leaf.

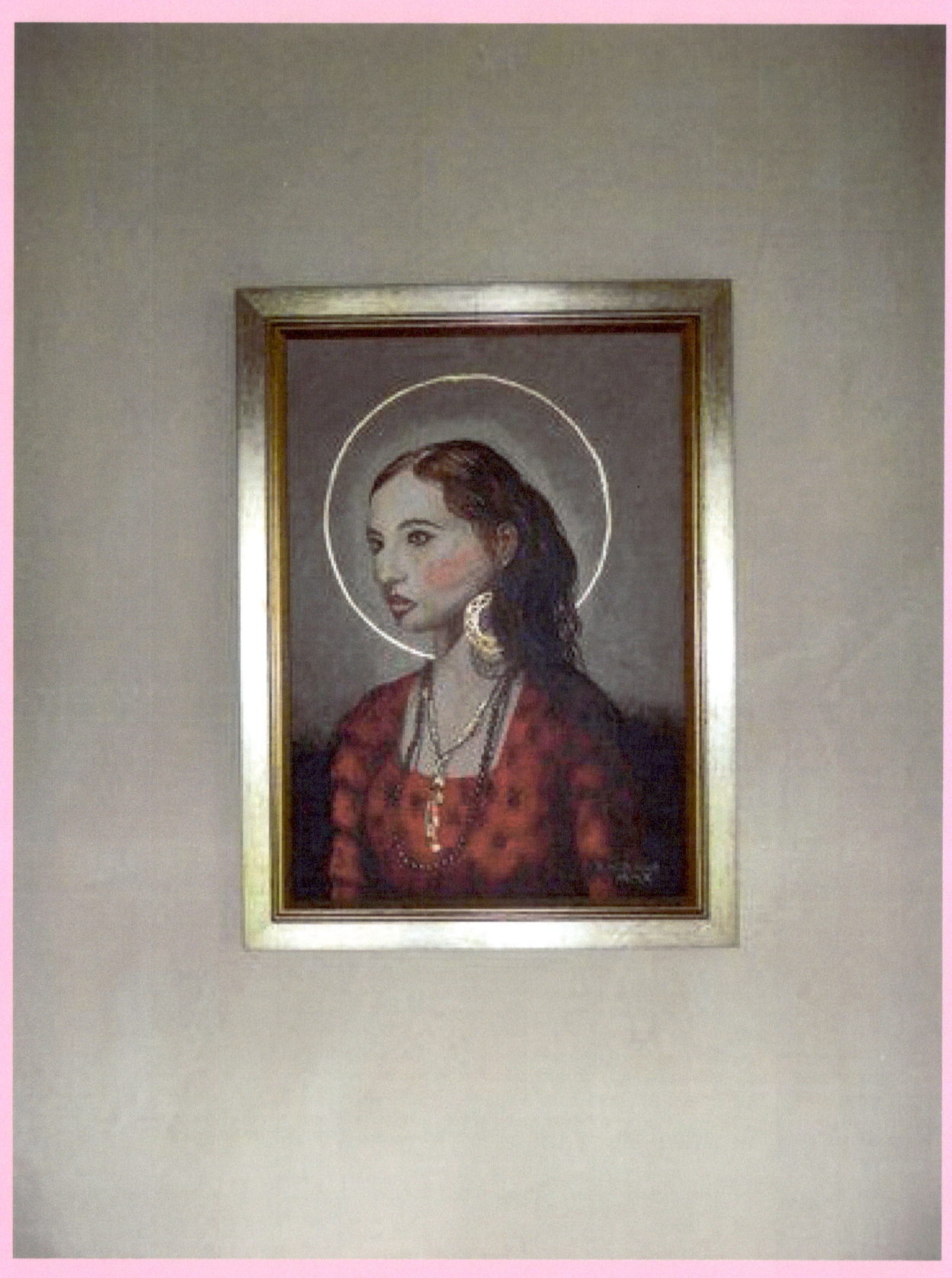

This portrait is my own creation, entitled 'Gipsy Madonna'.

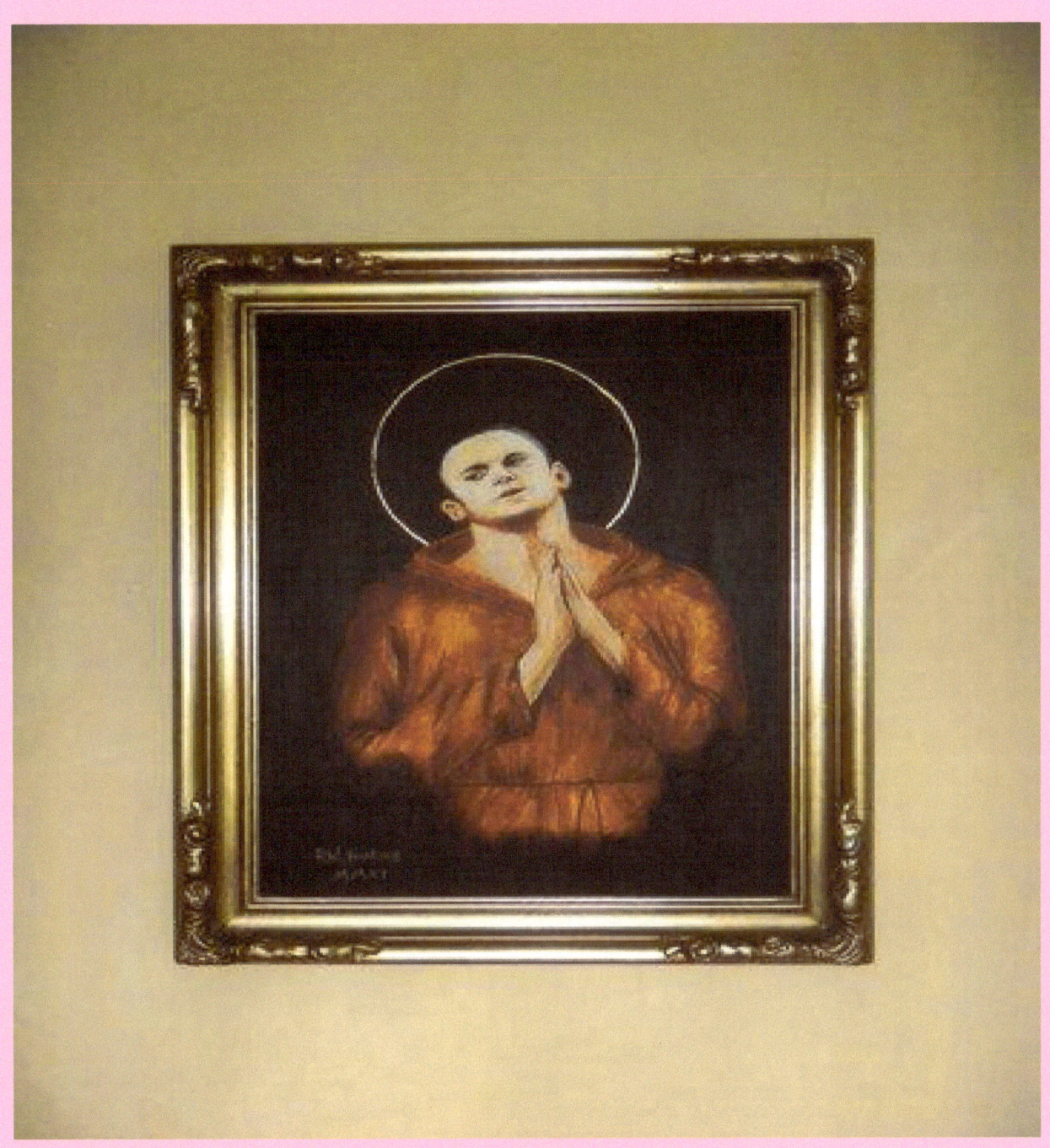

My own creation, entitled 'Saint Wayne of Old Trafford'. Wayne's pose was taken from the sports pages of a newspaper. He had just missed a shot on goal, and seems to be asking for divine intervention, in a manner similar to that shown in Francisco de Zurbaran's 'Saint Francis in Meditation', which is represented elsewhere in this book. Wayne is built like a mountain, but has such delicate hands.

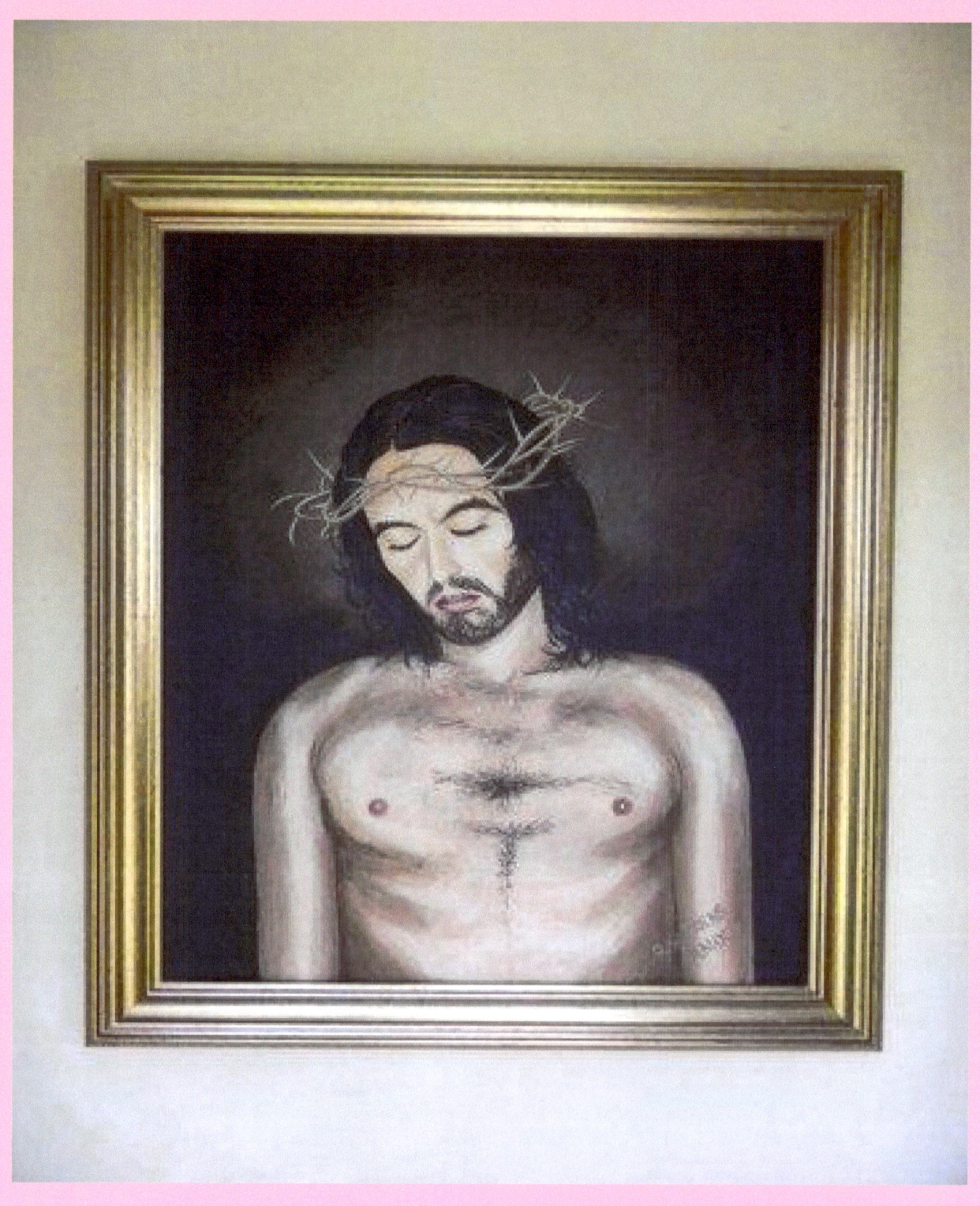

My own creation, entitled 'Russell Brand - Crown of Thorns'. Should there ever be a remake of 'Jesus of Nazareth', Russell would be ideal for the title role. He looks the part - tall, black hair and beard, emaciated, and is the most erudite young man of his generation.

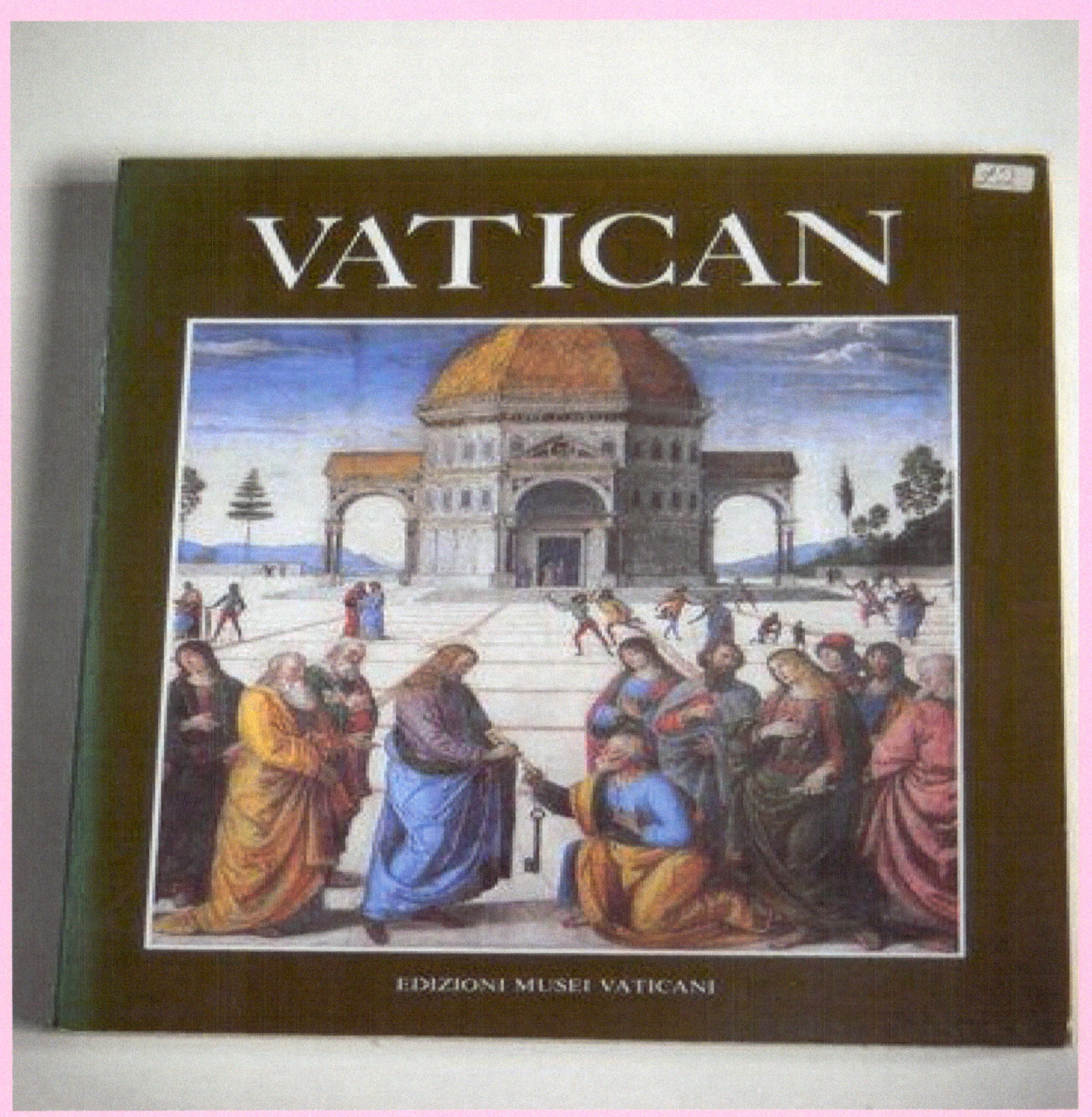

The Renaissance House would not exist without this book, which sparked my interest in Renaissance art, and inspired me to paint. I bought this 1993 tourist guide for £2 at a car boot sale. Previously, I had seen pictures of Rome's Sistine Chapel and Saint Peter's Basilica, but had no idea of the true extent of Renaissance art on display at the Vatican. The guide prompted me to acquire further books, thereby increasing my knowledge of Renaissance art, before beginning to paint the house.

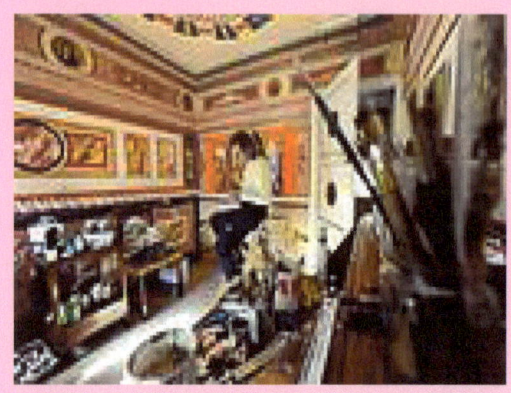
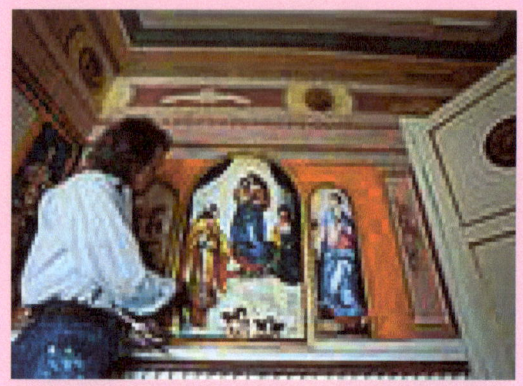
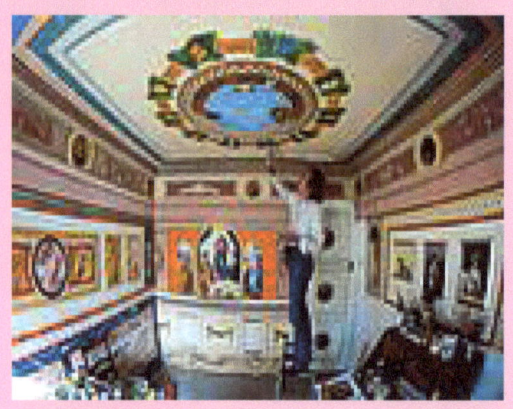
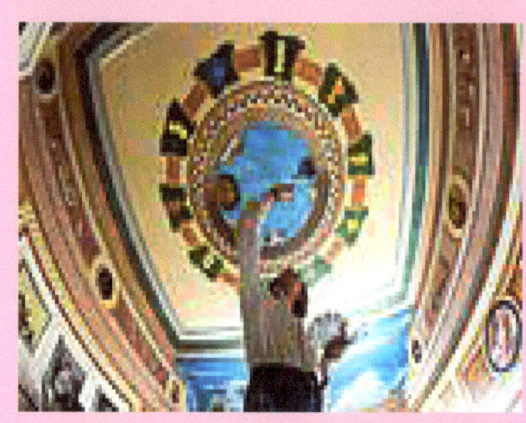
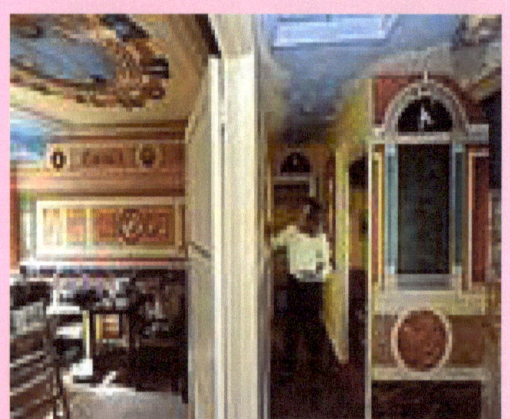
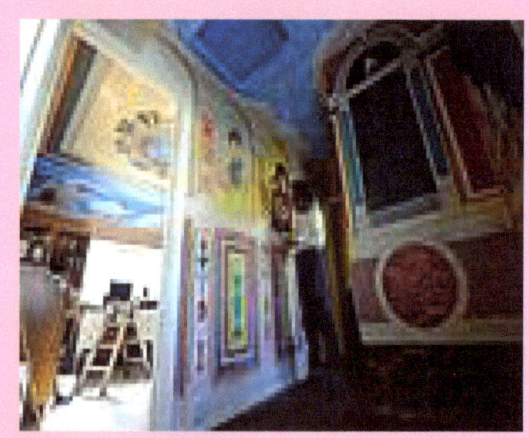
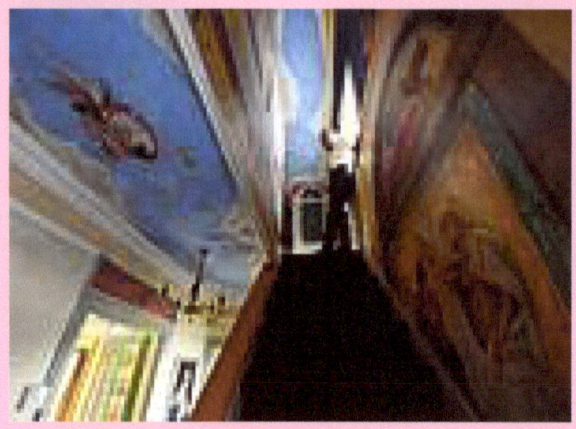

Artist Robert W. Burns at work.

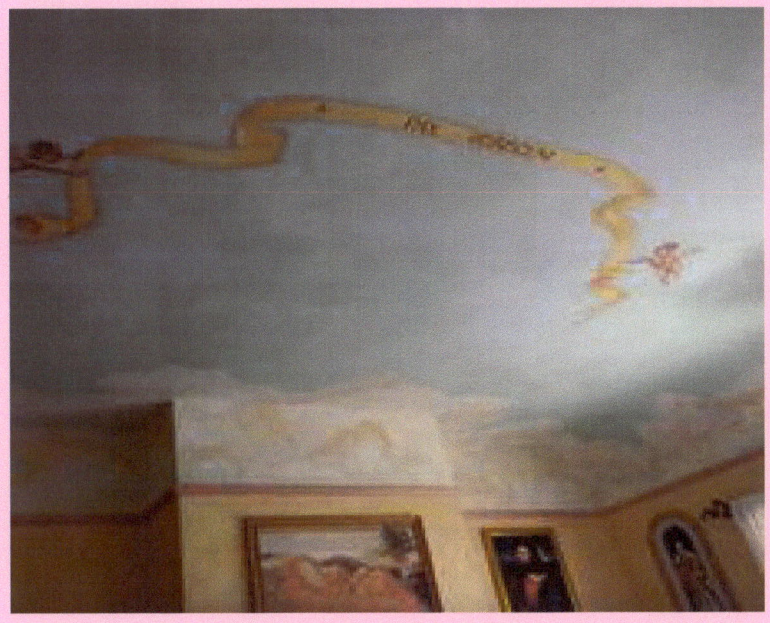

Here's a nice way to finish this book. The Latin inscription on the bedroom ceiling reads 'pax vobiscum' - peace (be) with you.